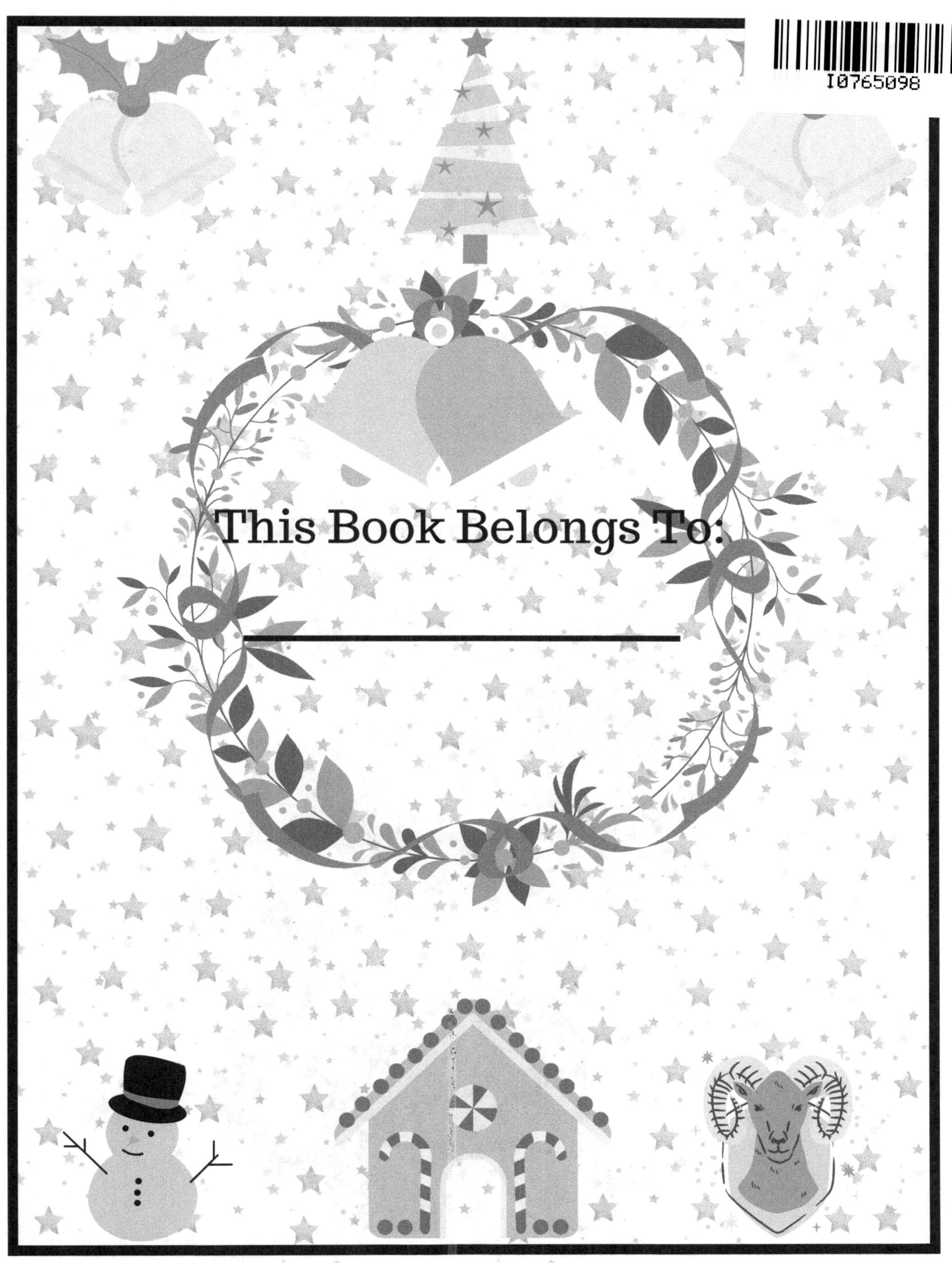

This Book Belongs To:

CHRISTMAS COLOURING BOOK
KIDS

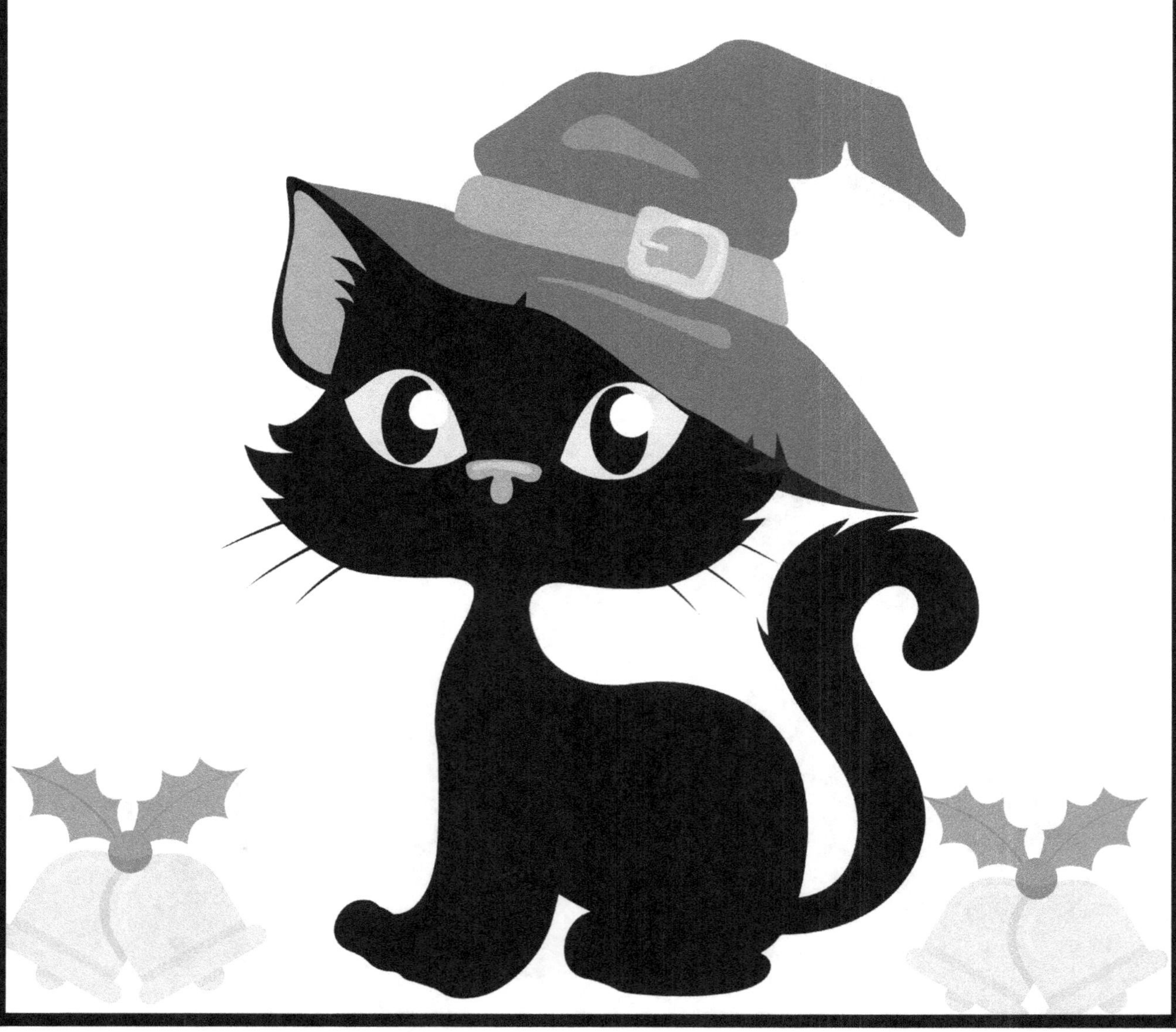

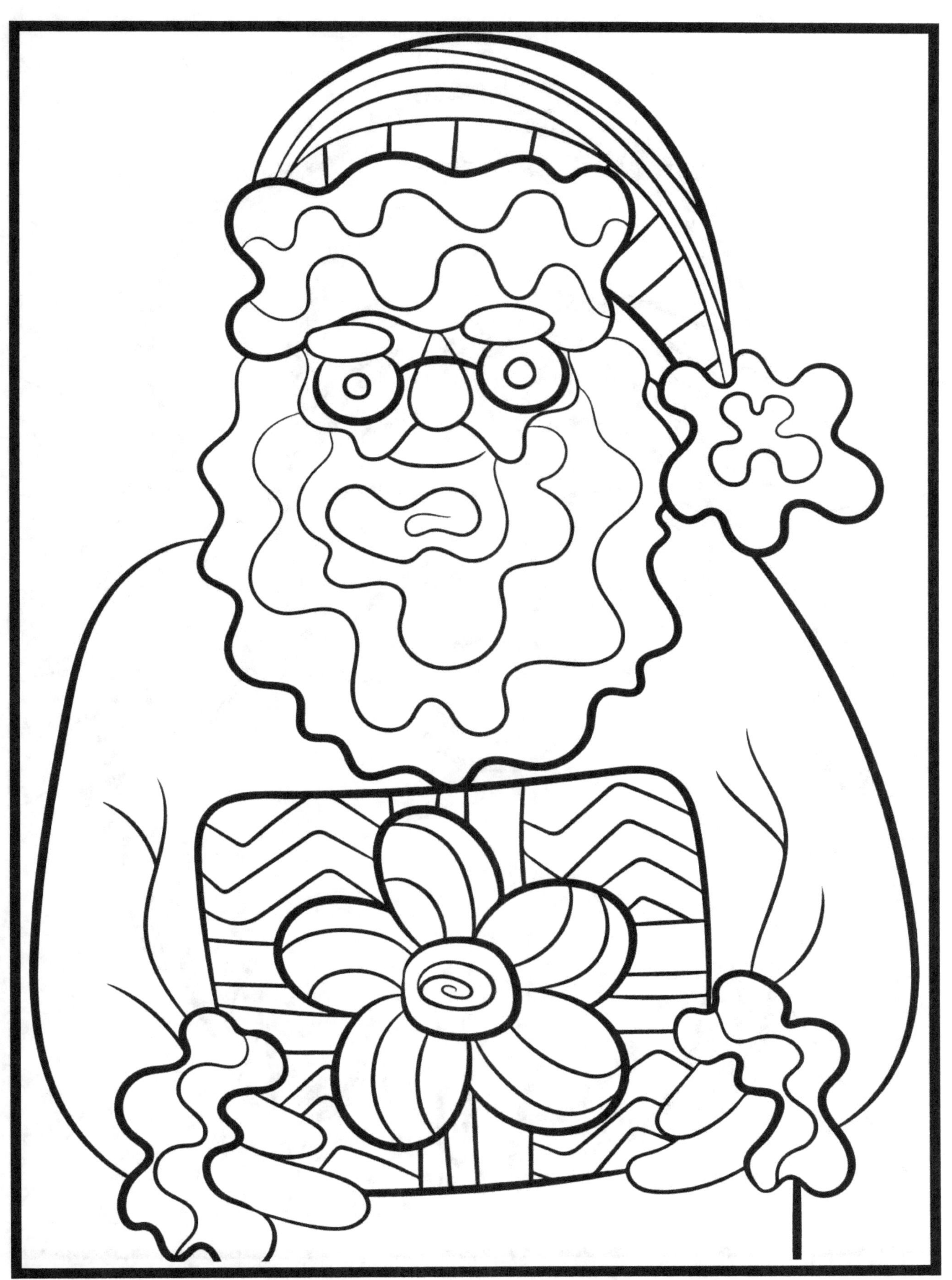

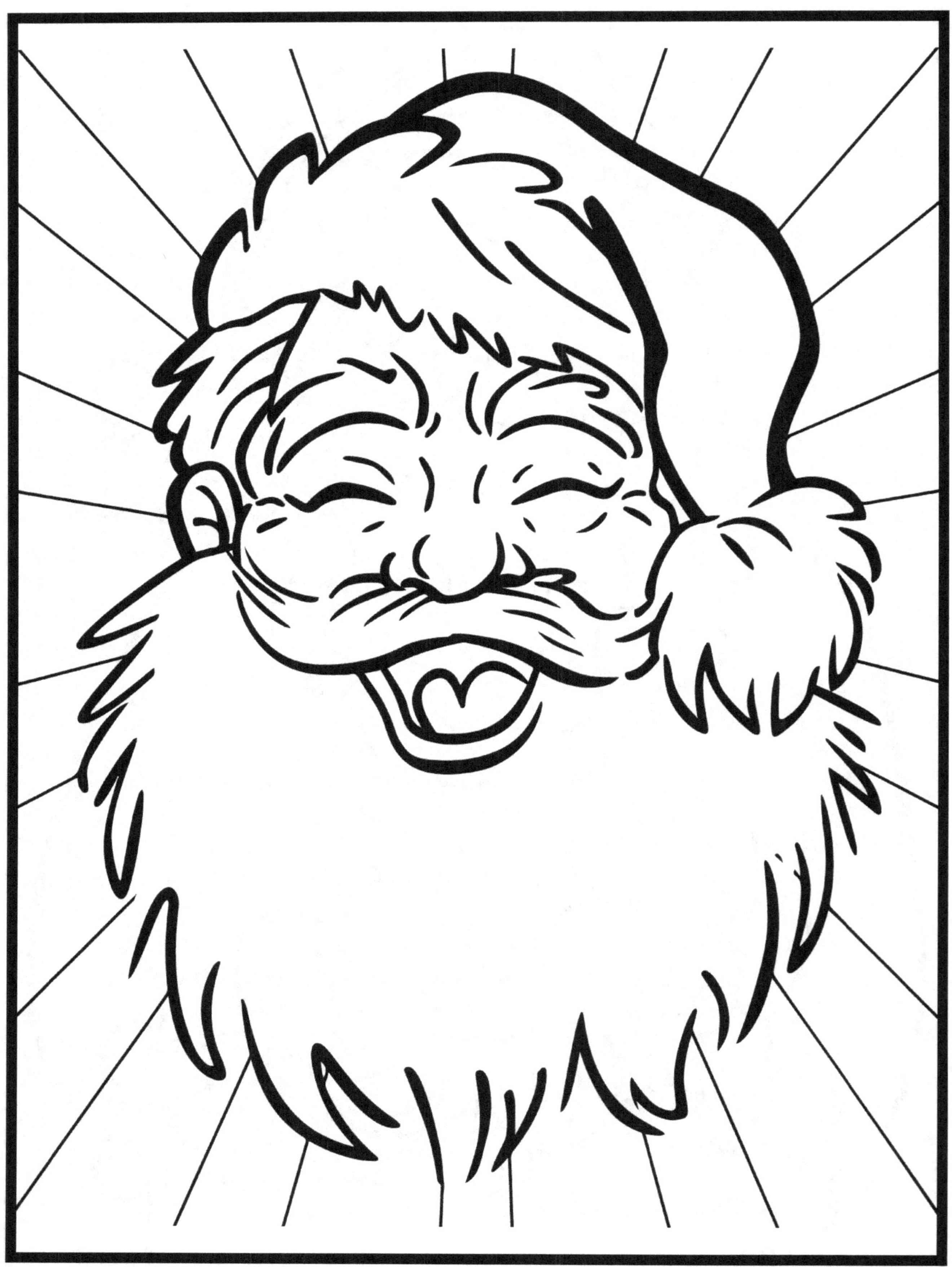

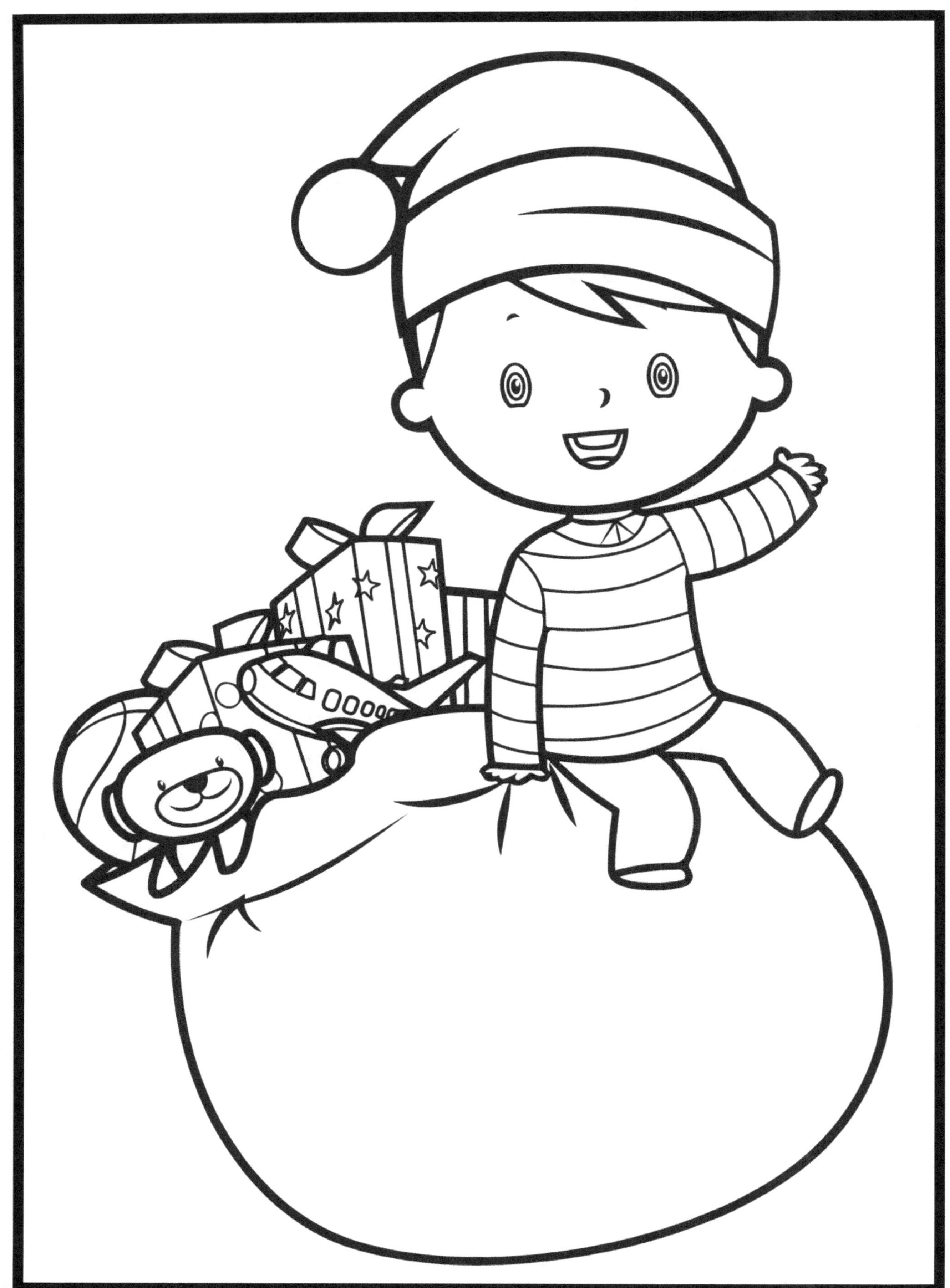

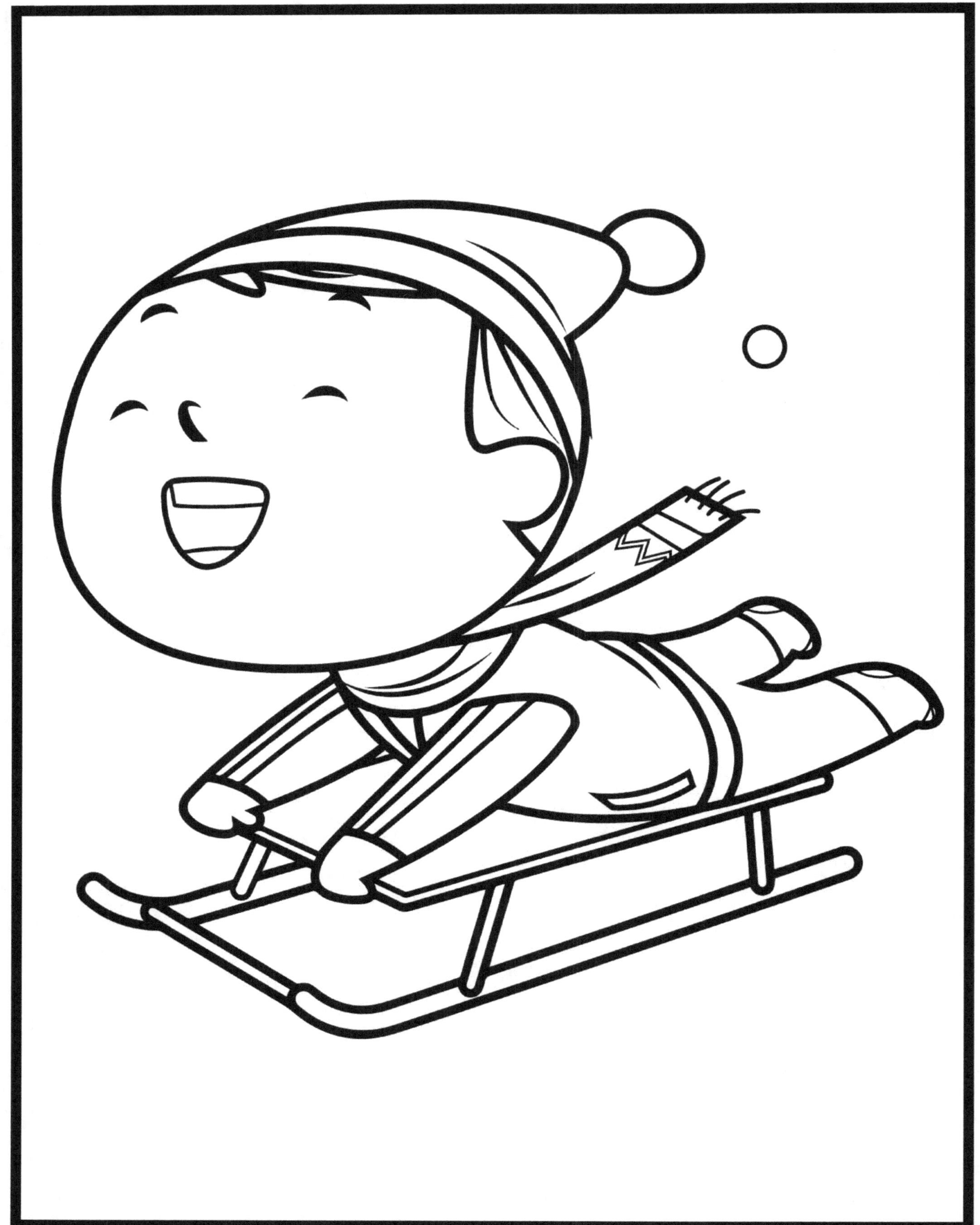

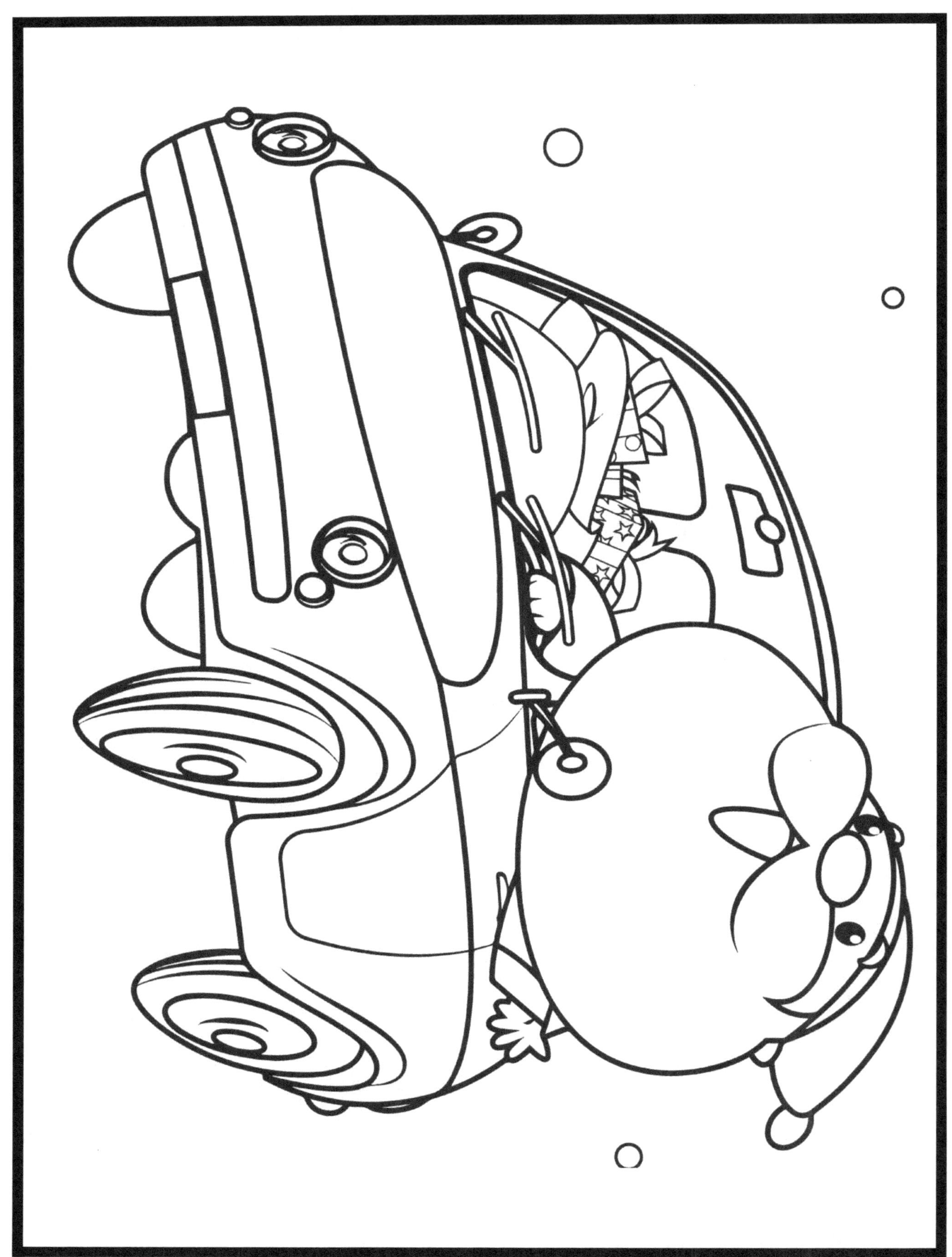

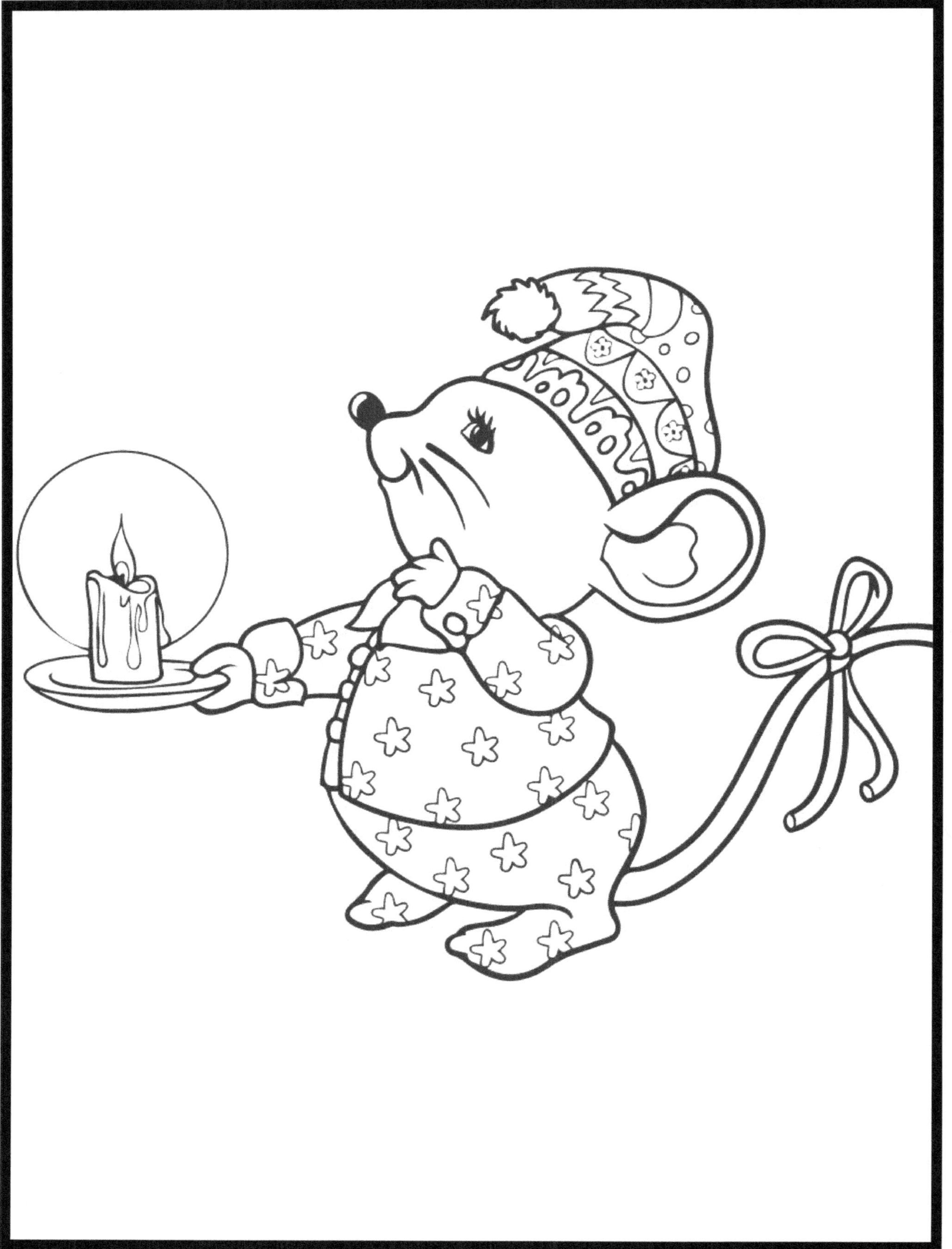

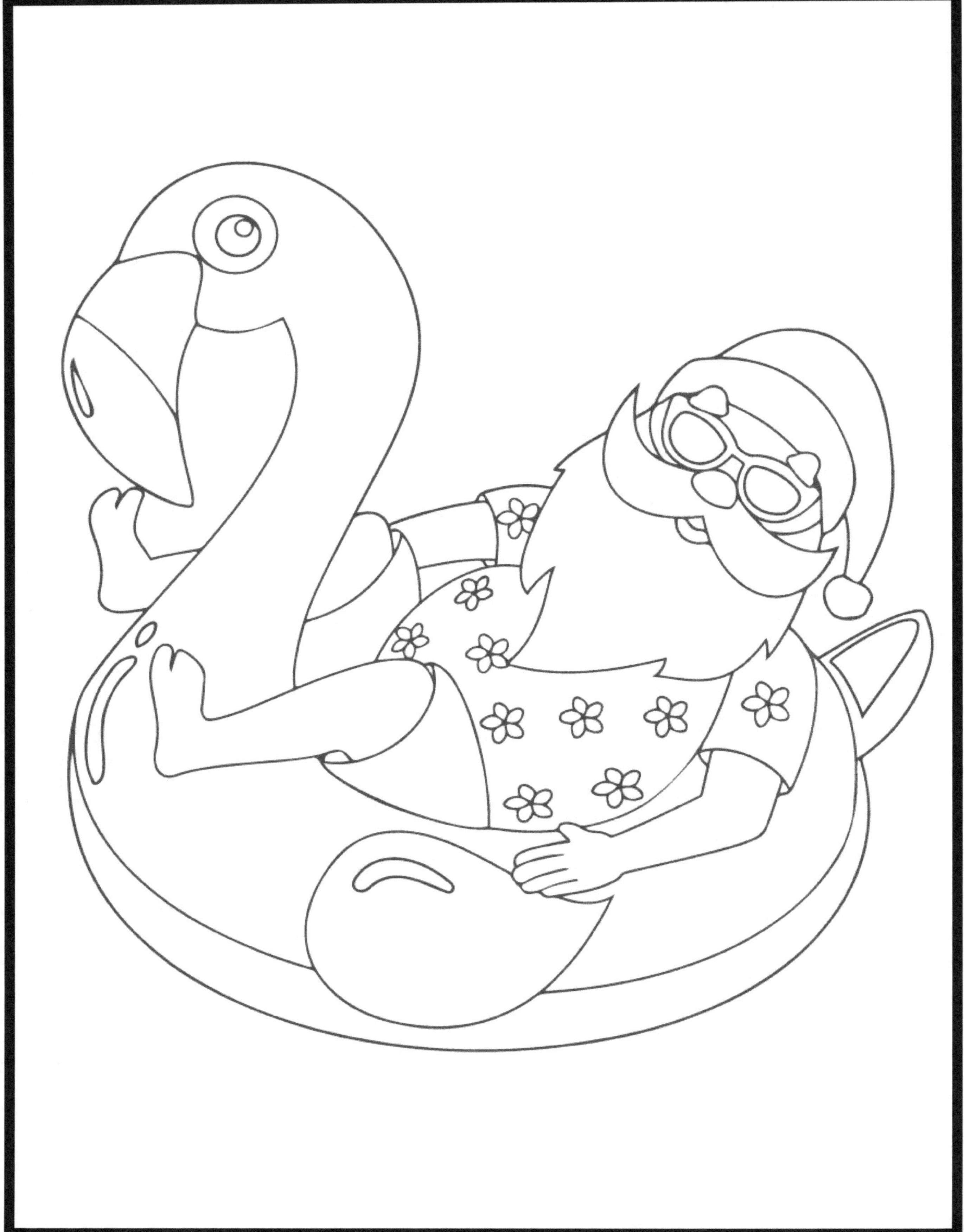

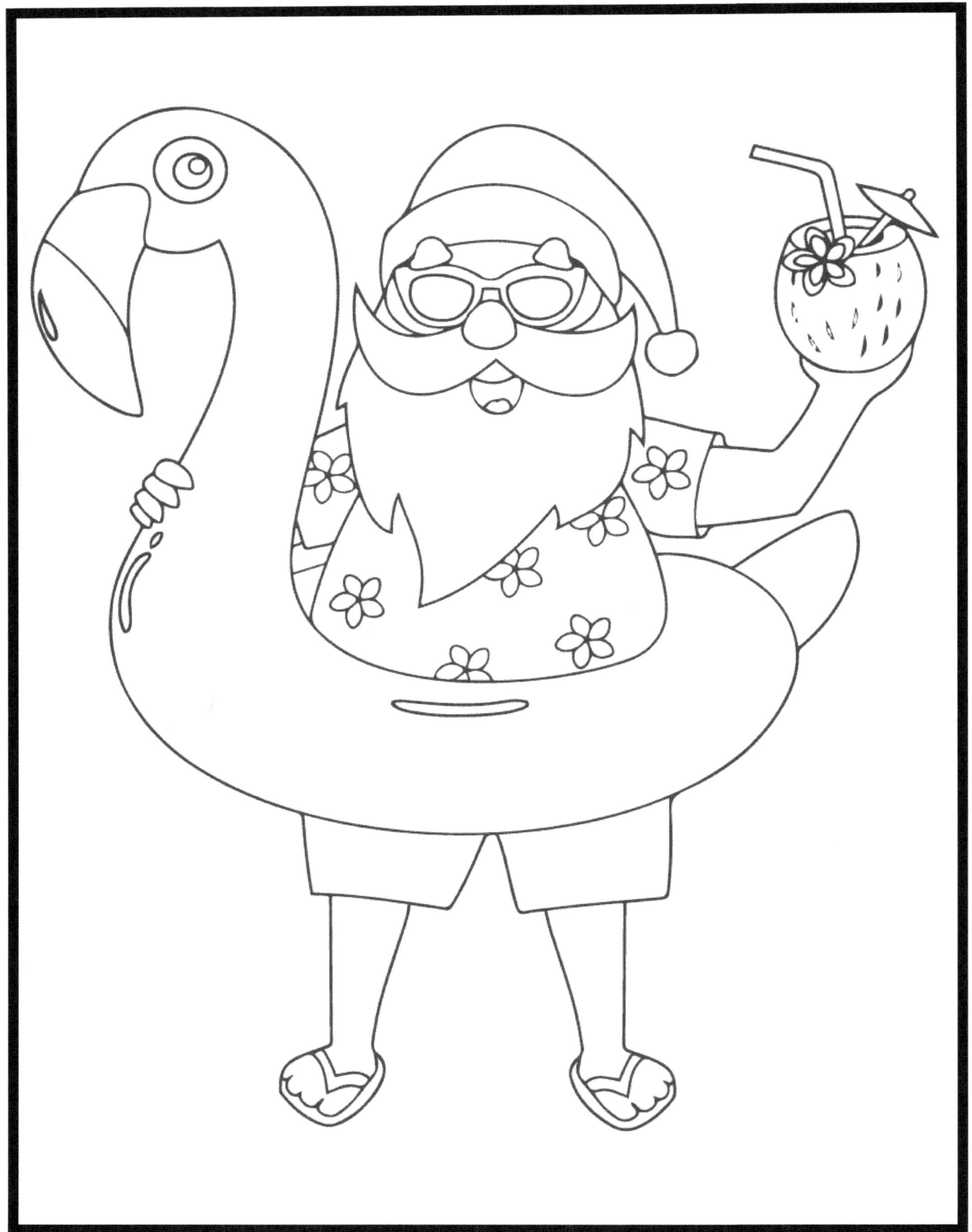

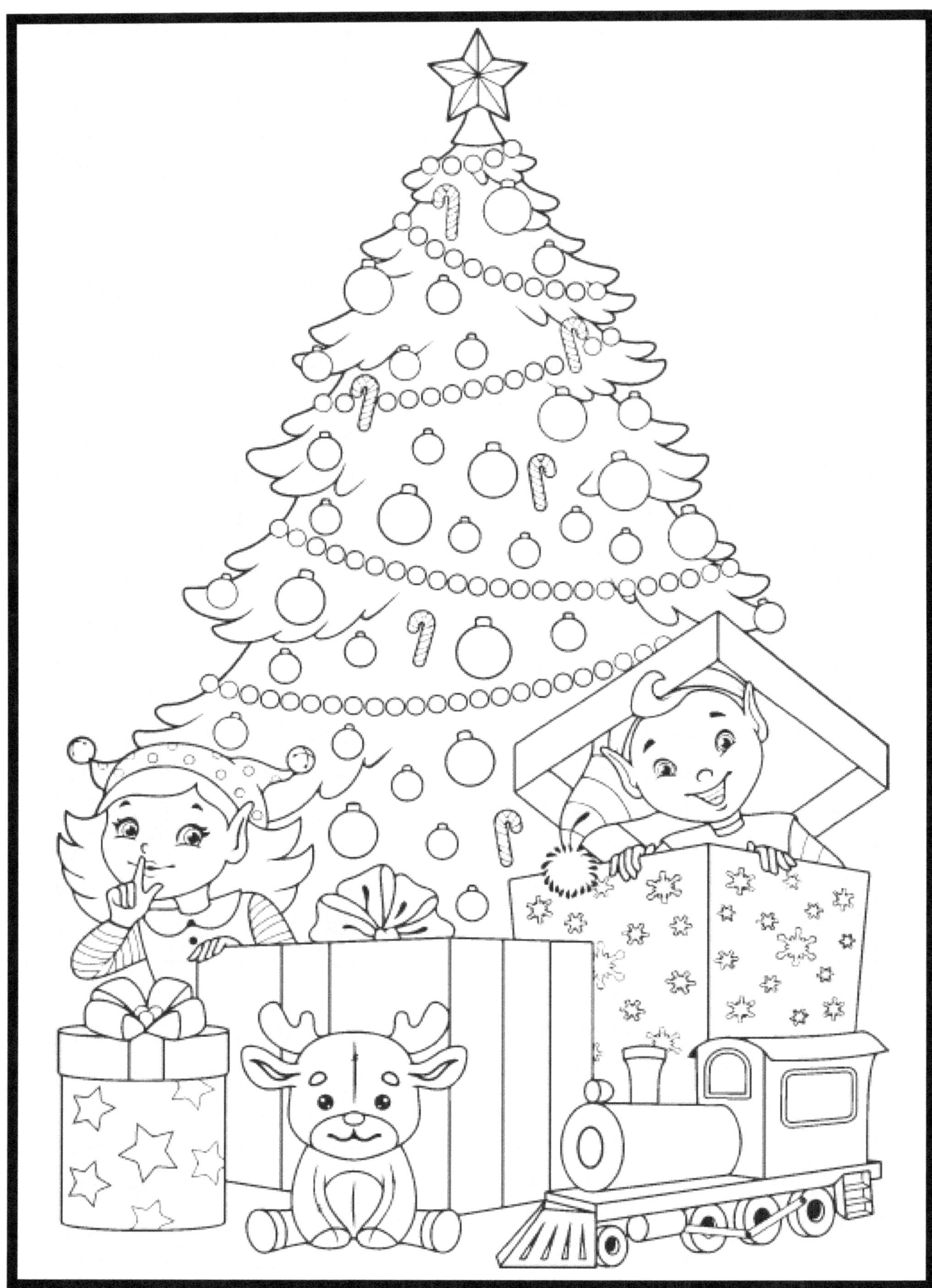

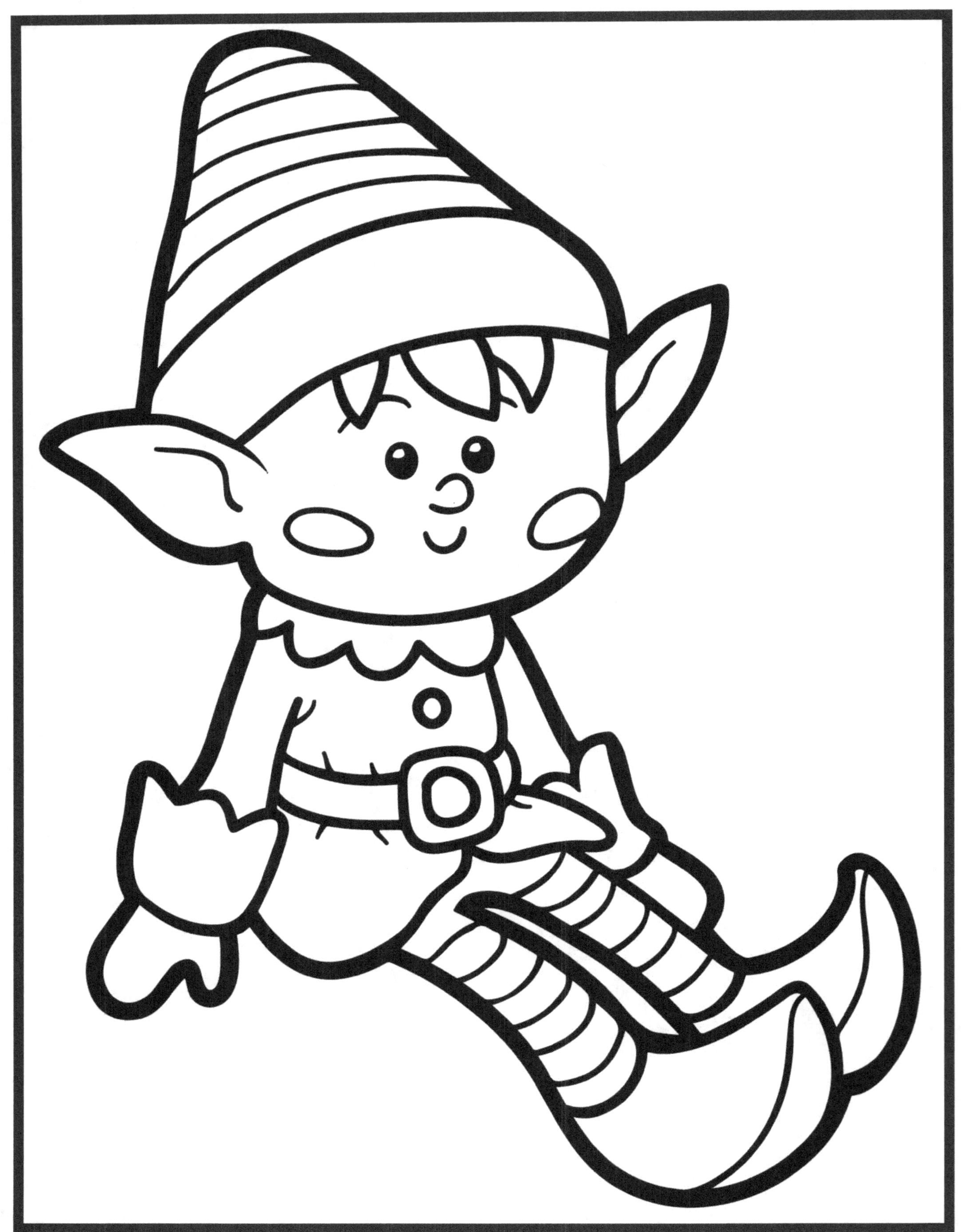

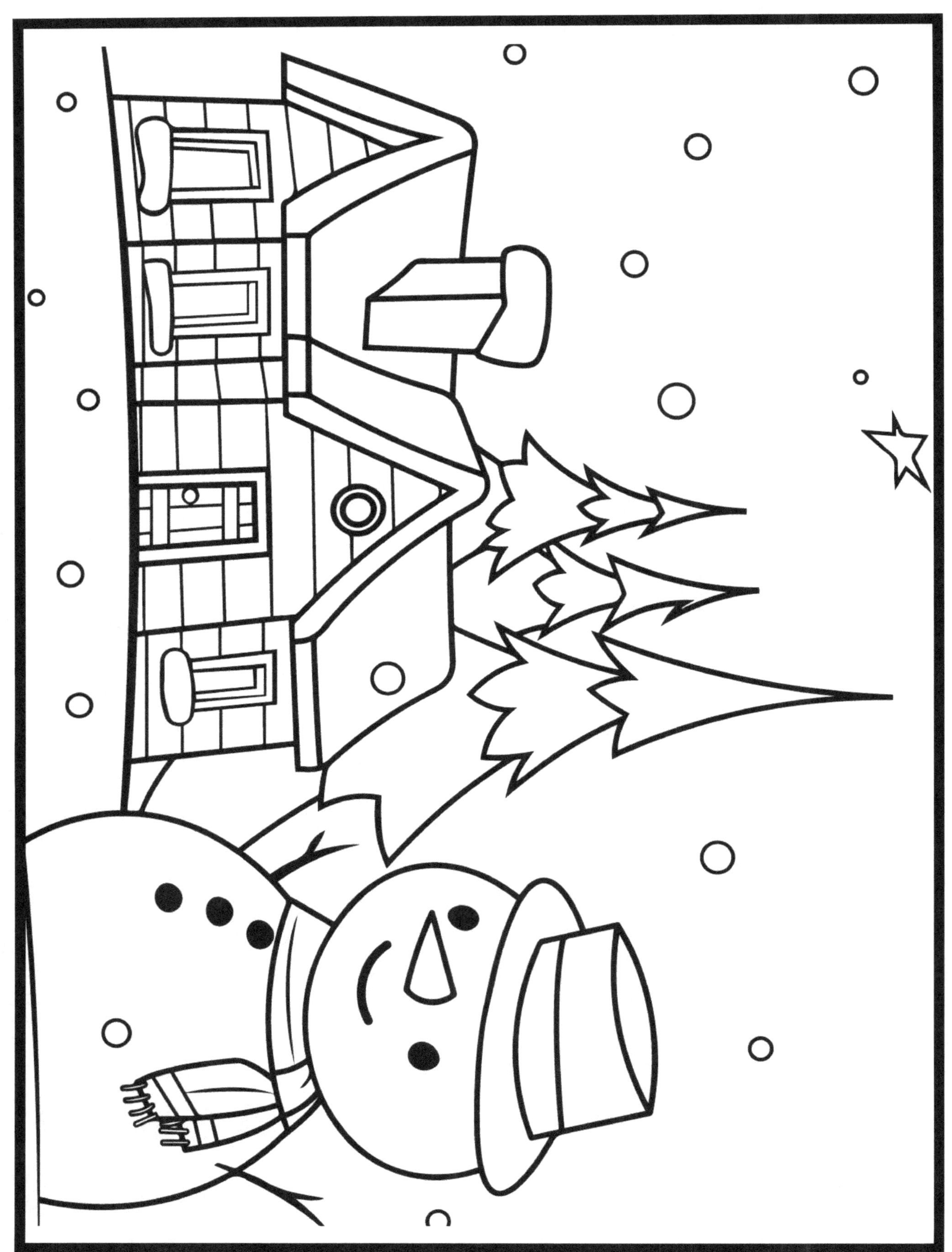

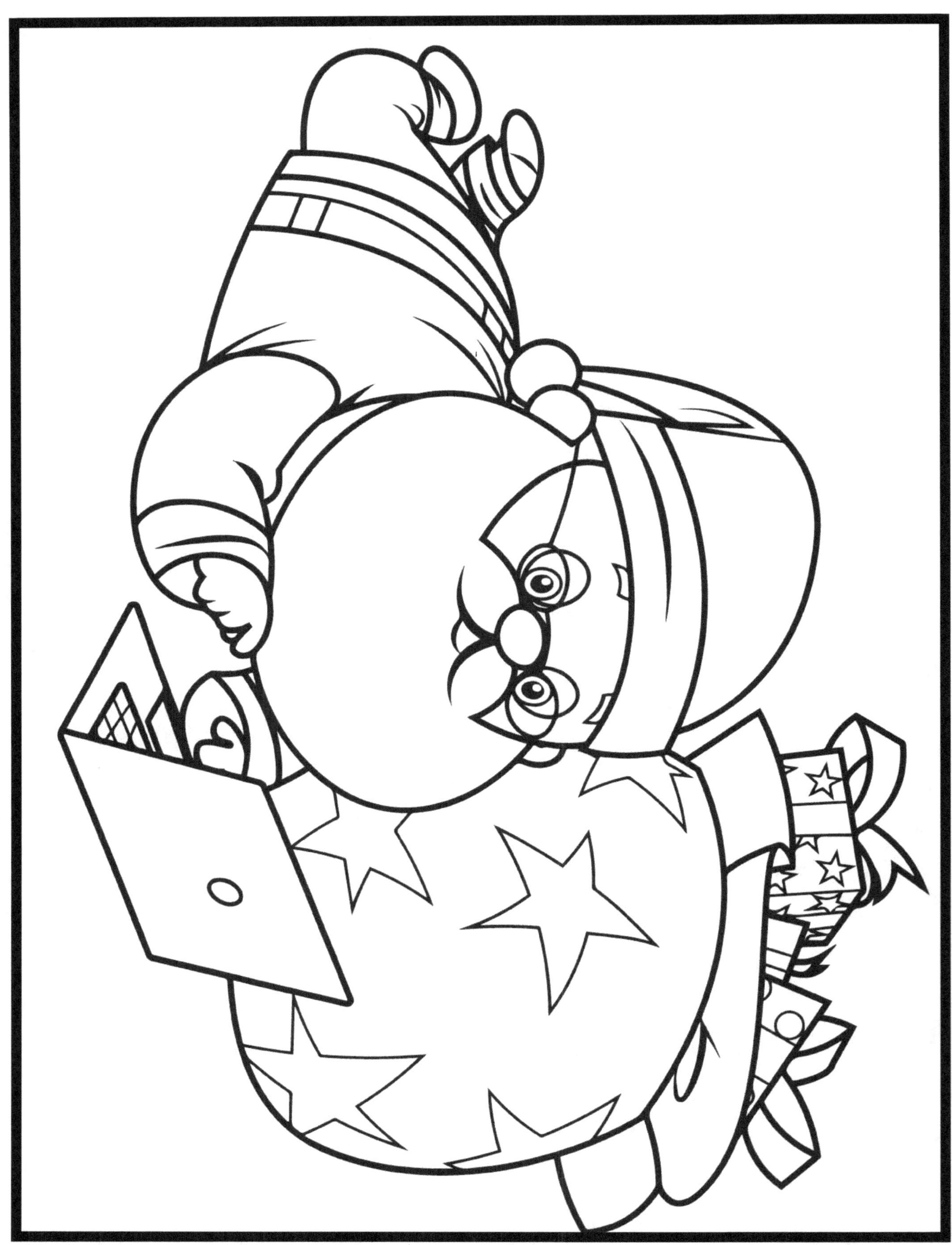

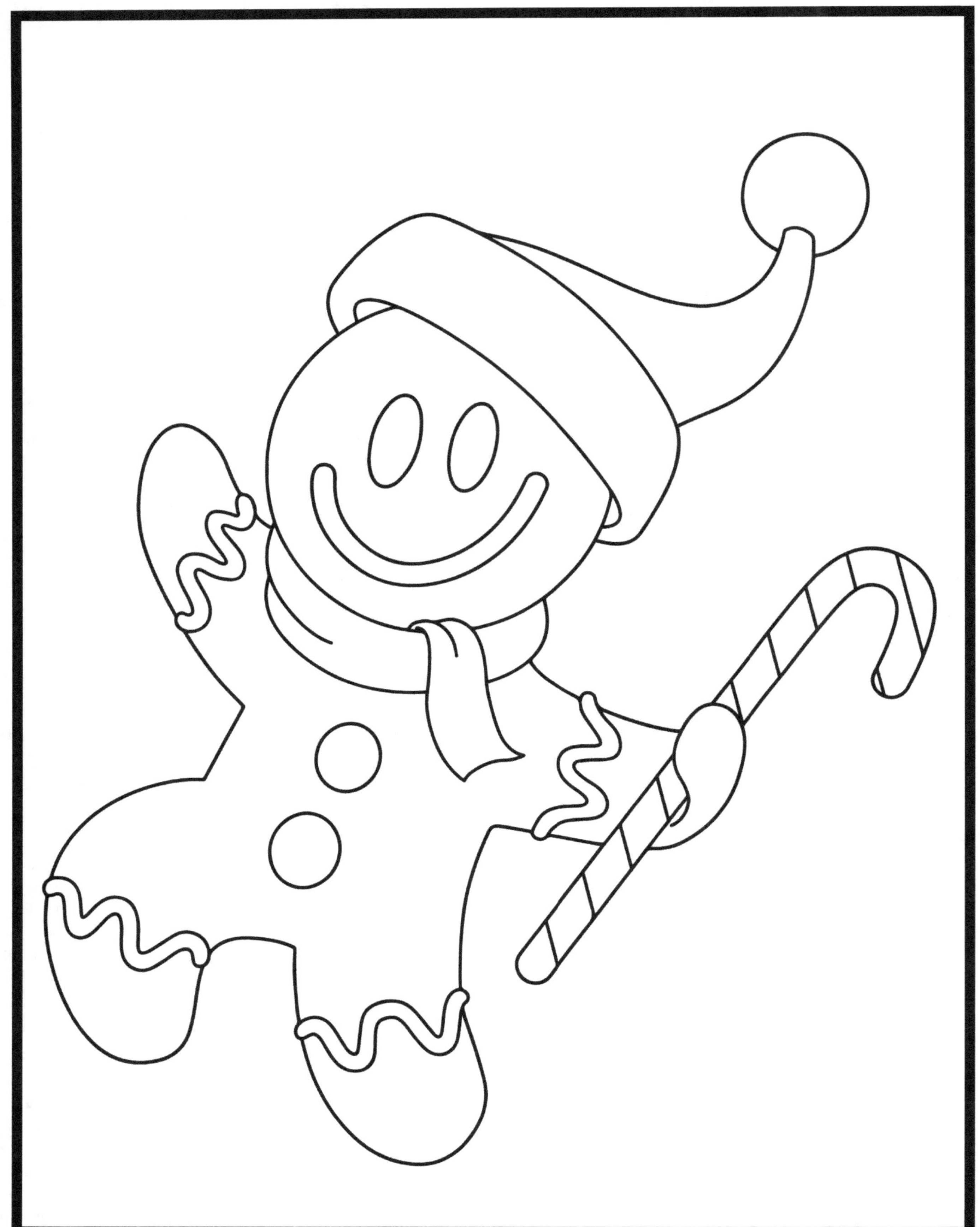

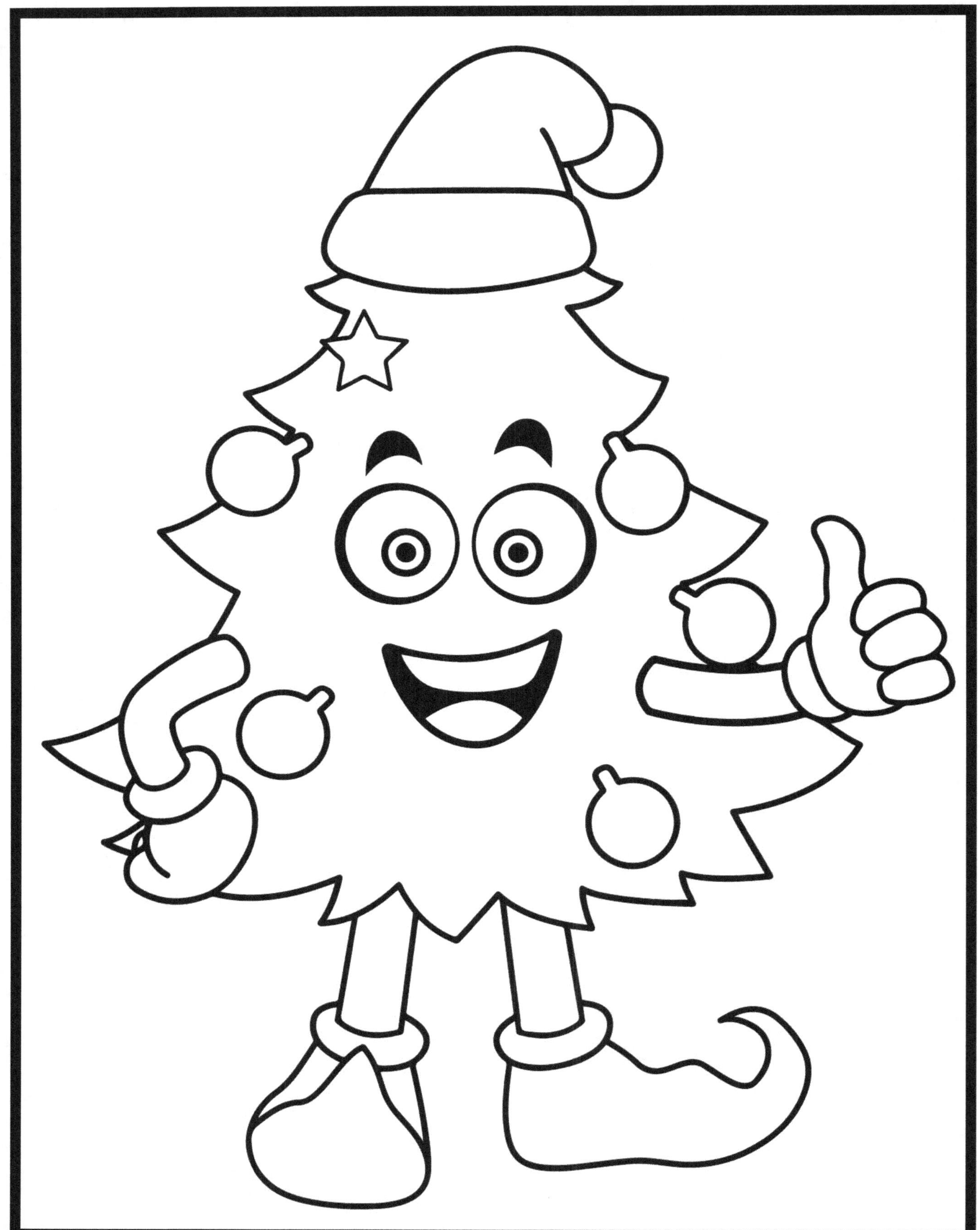

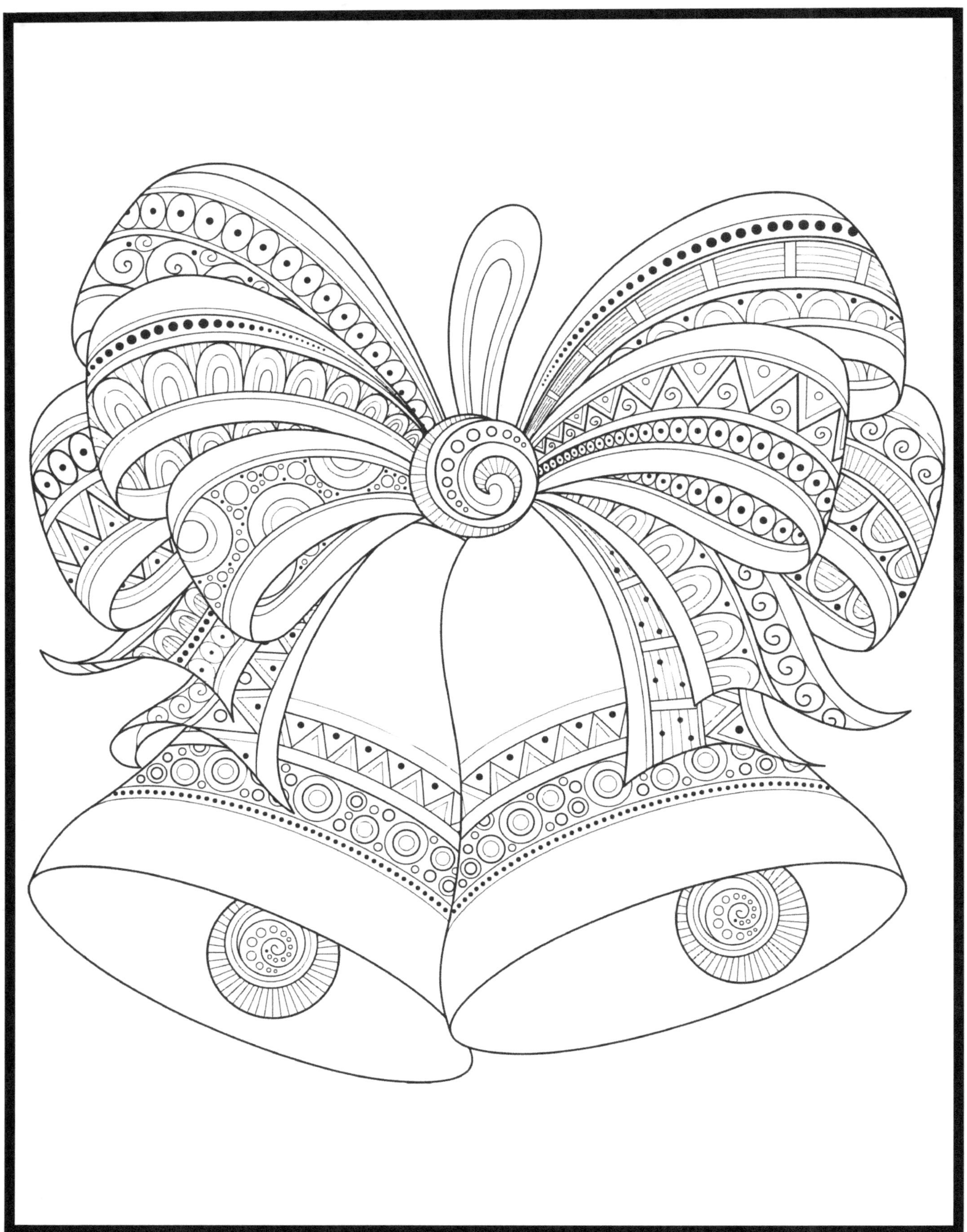

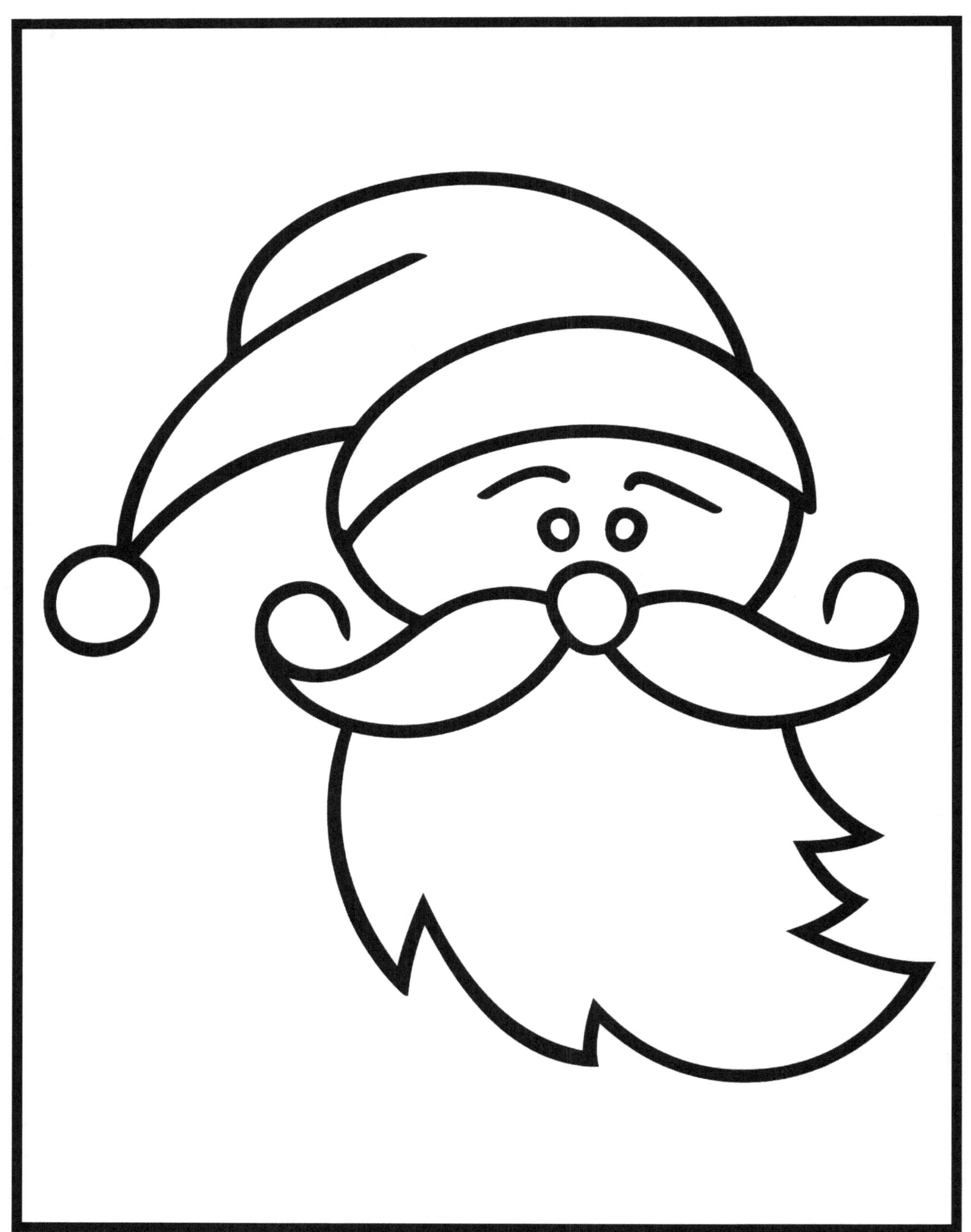

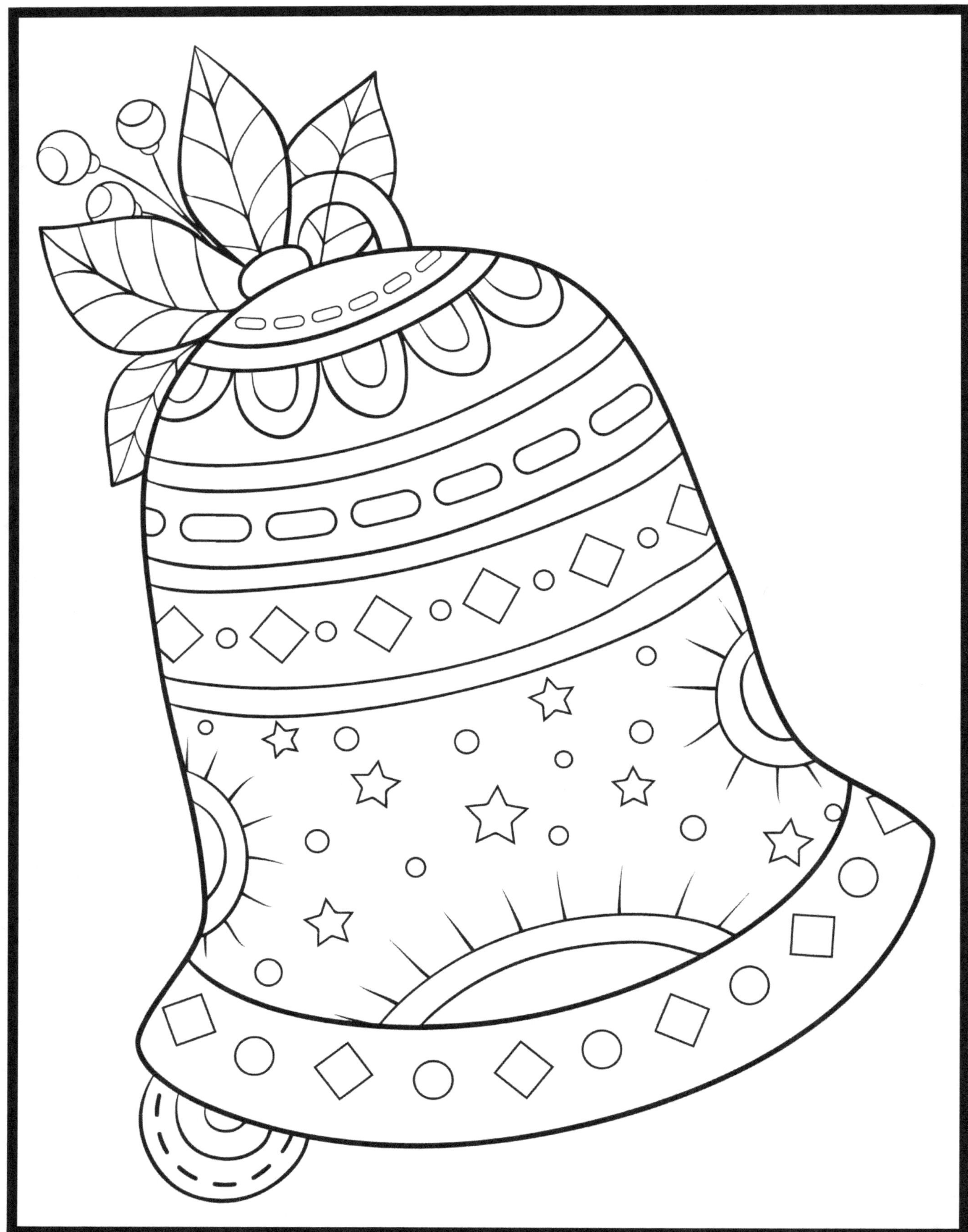

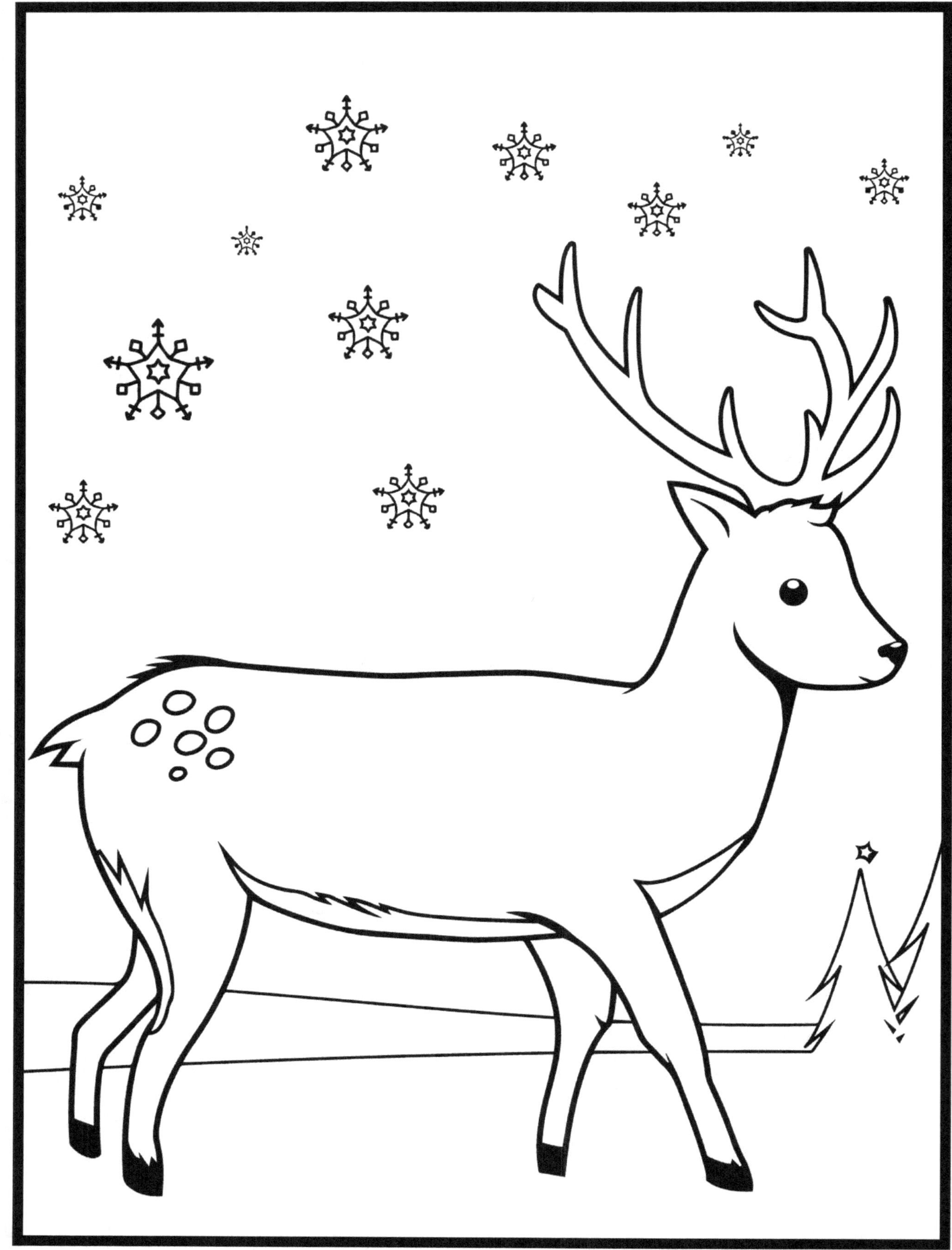

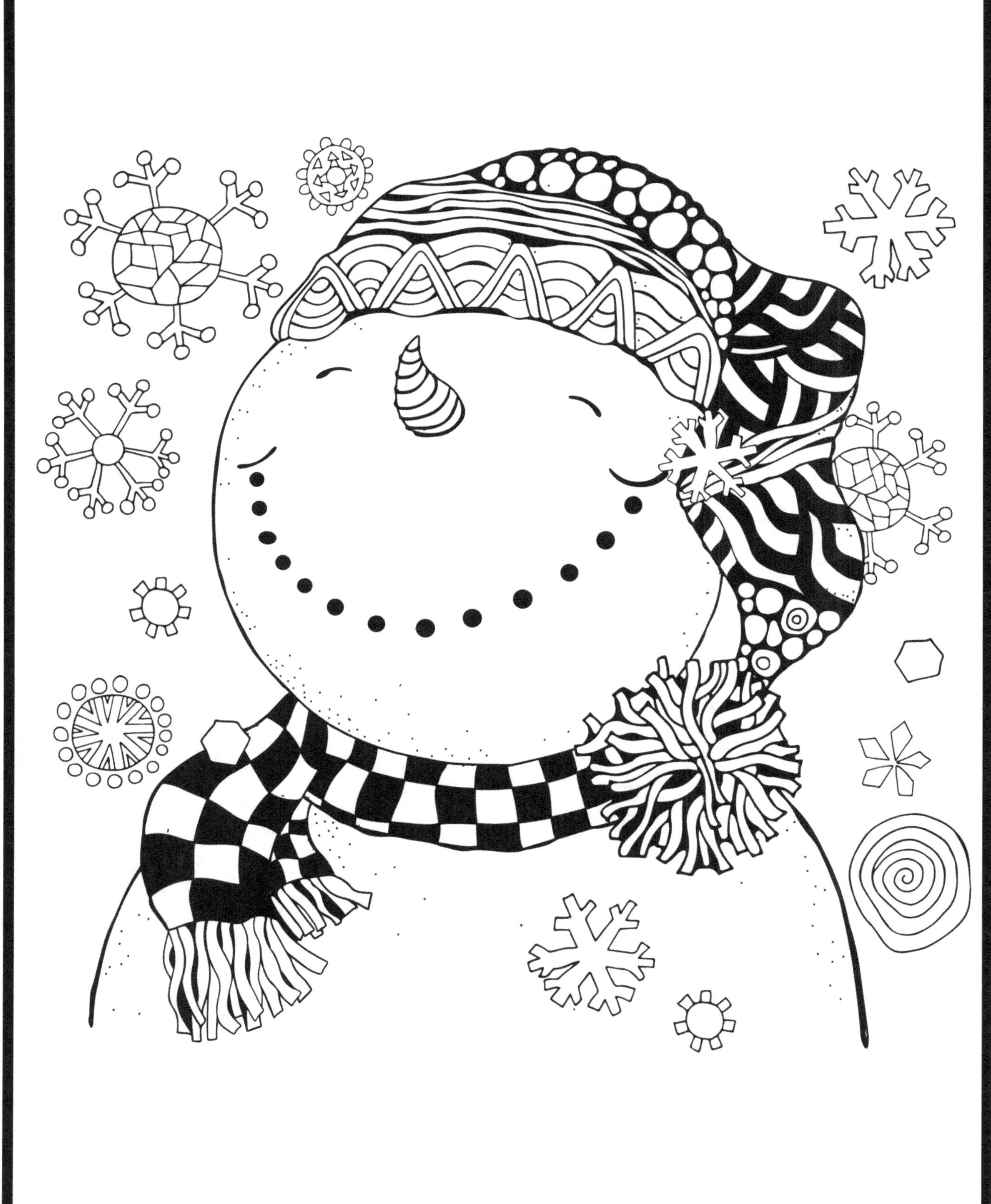

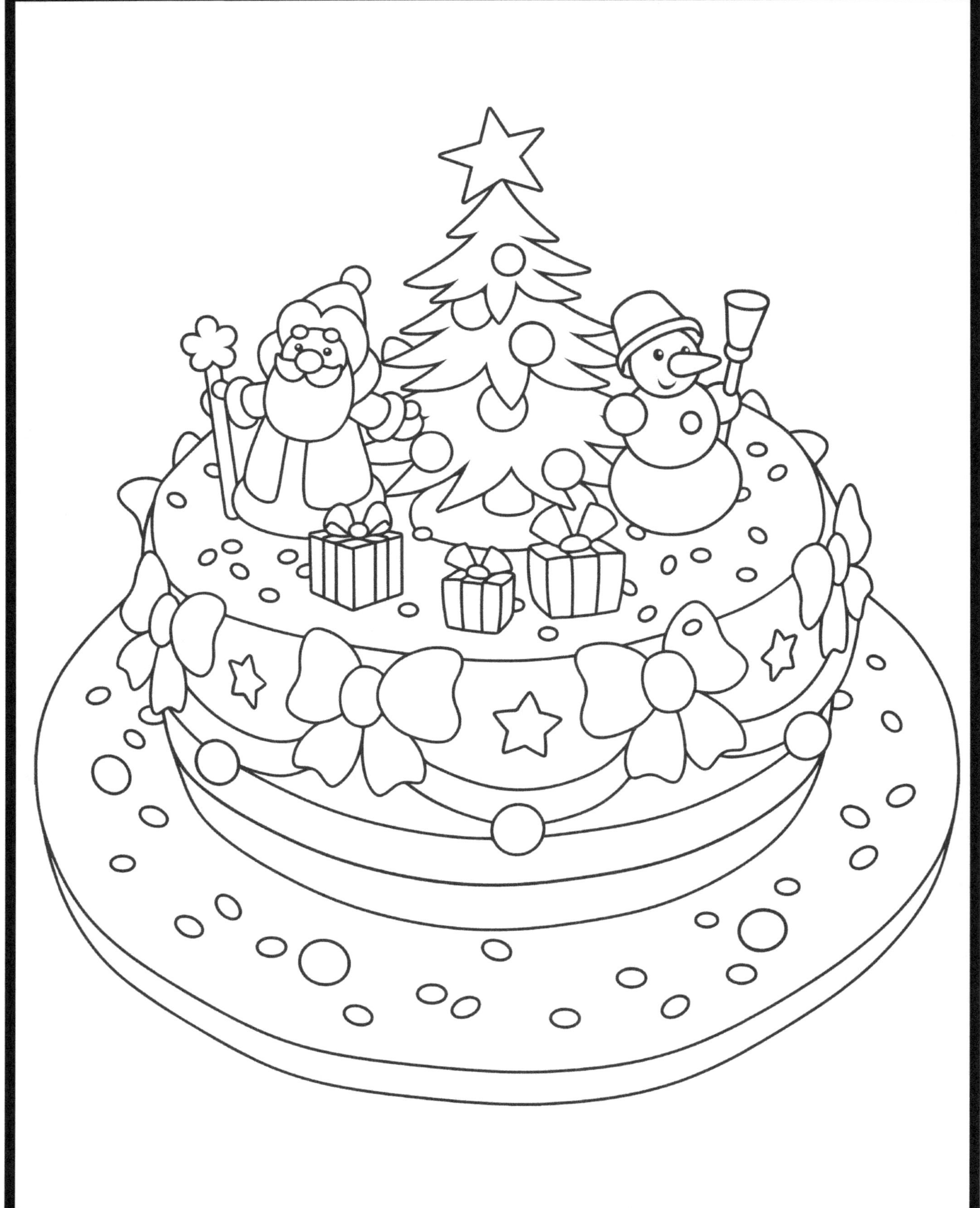

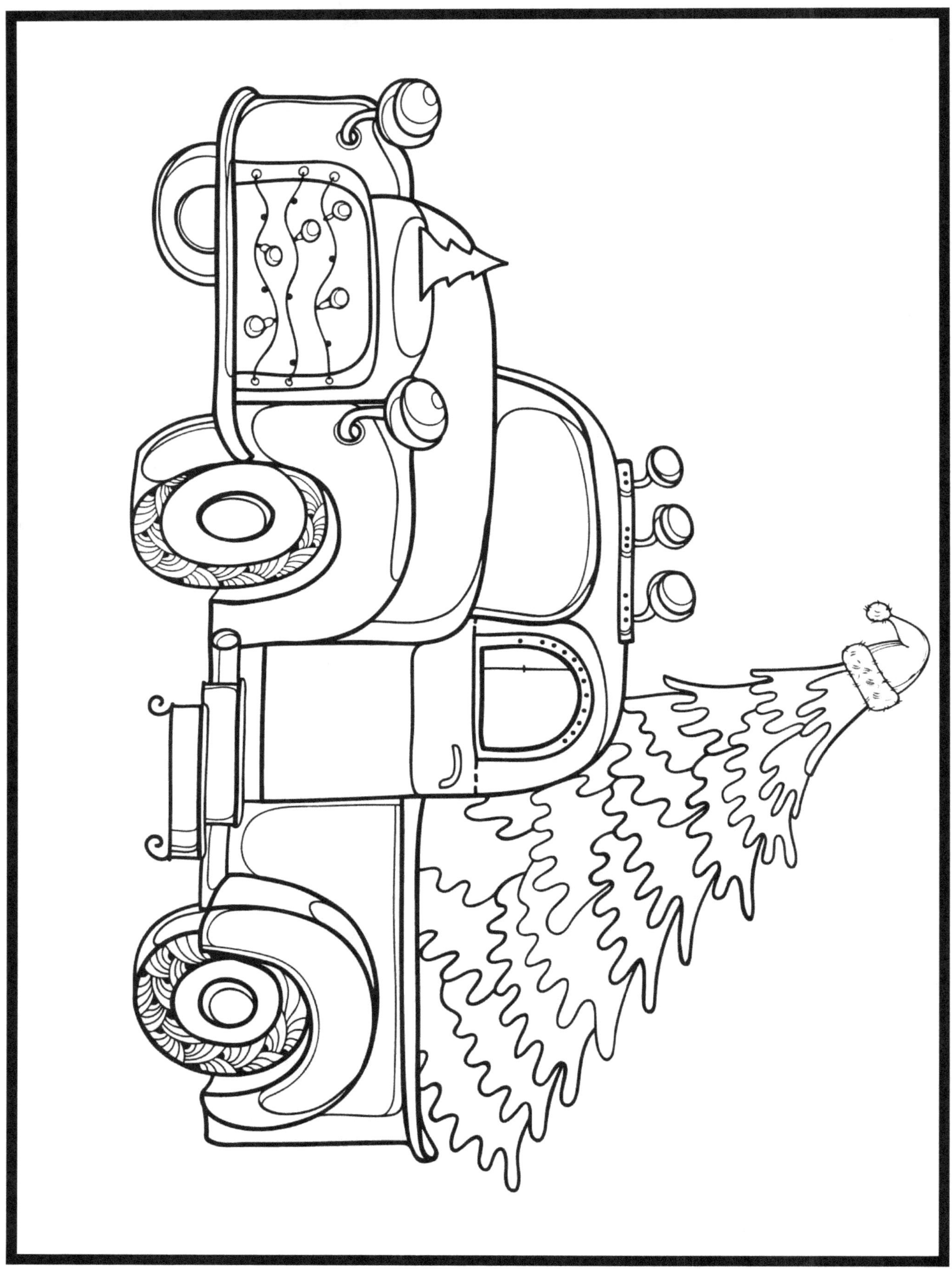

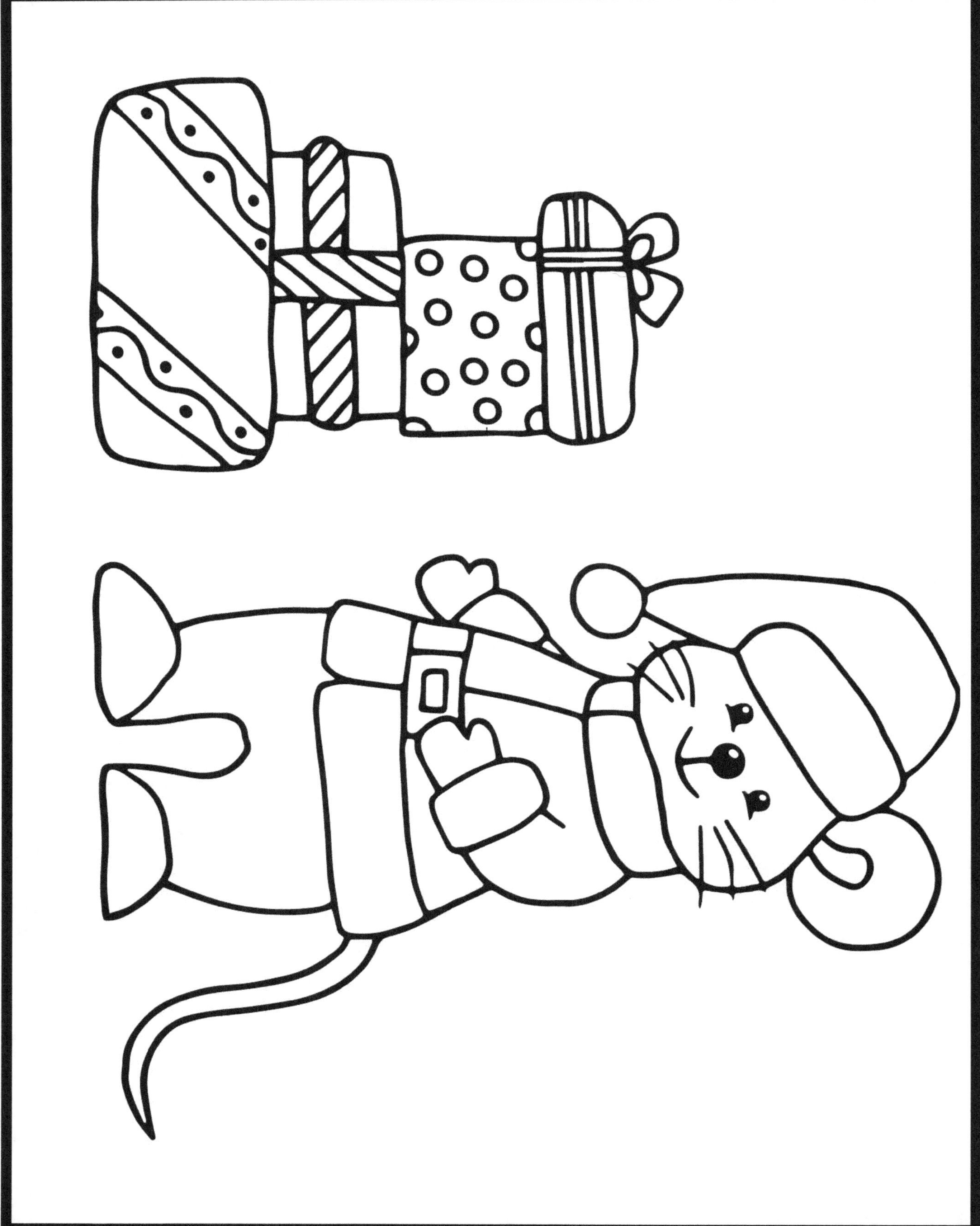

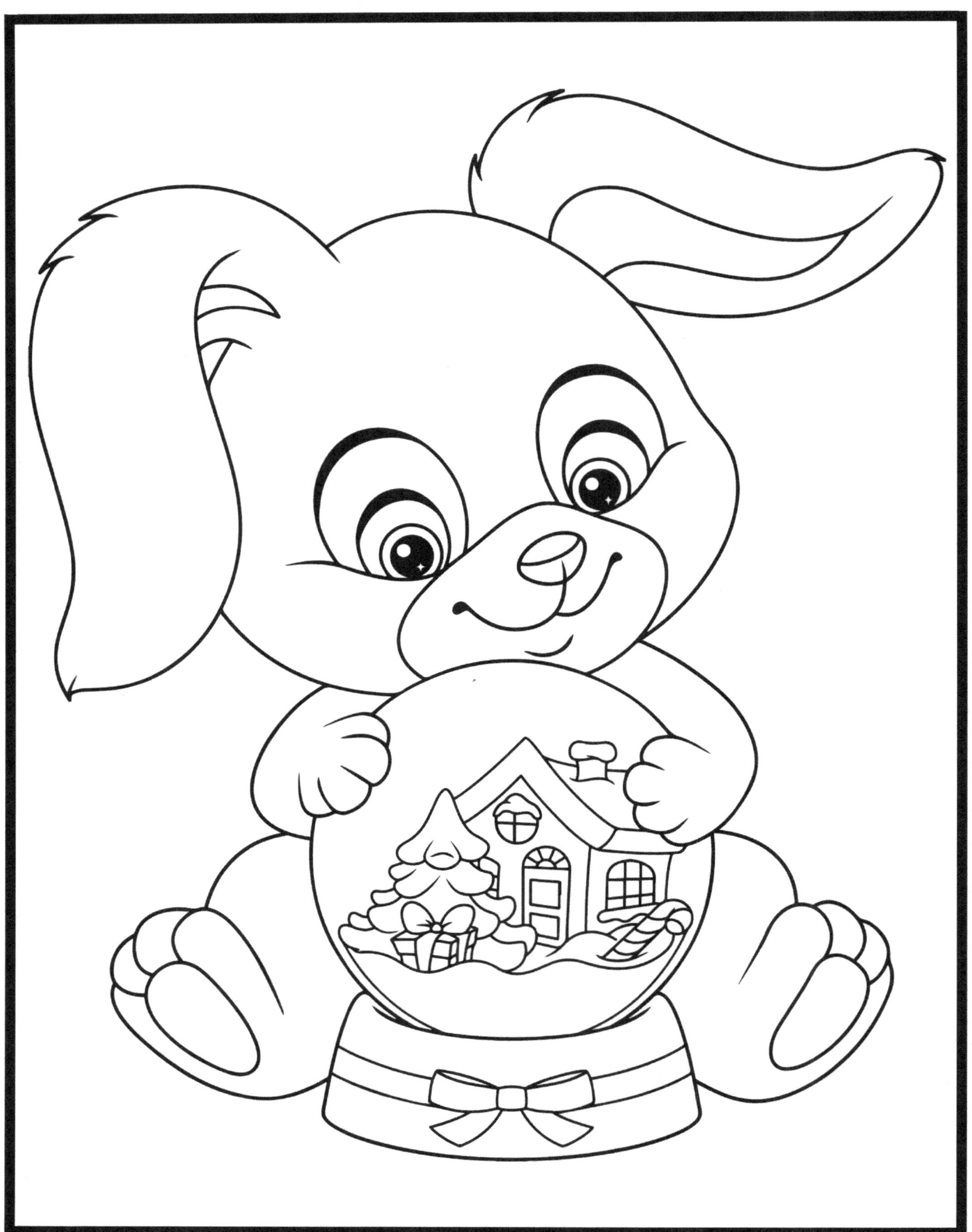

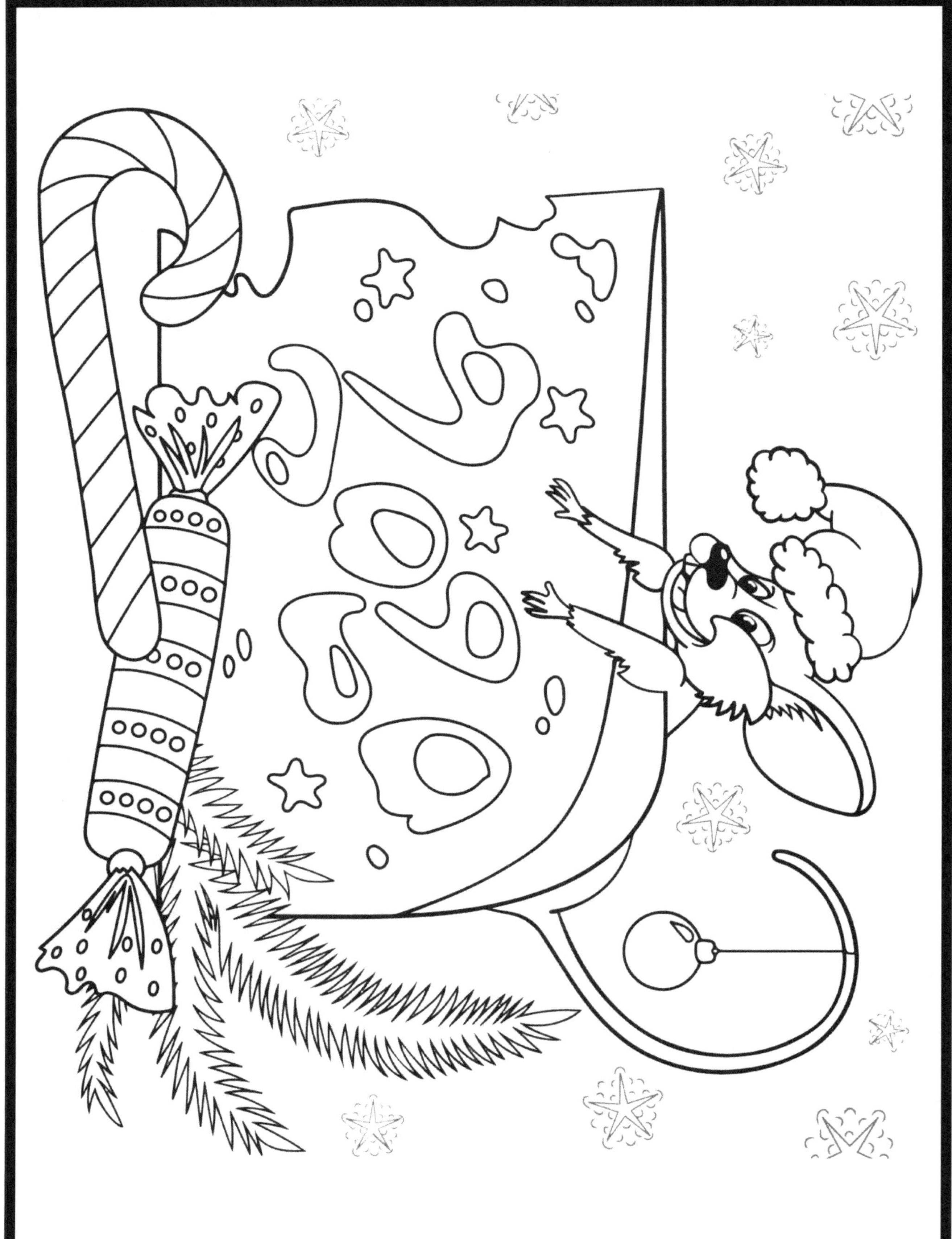

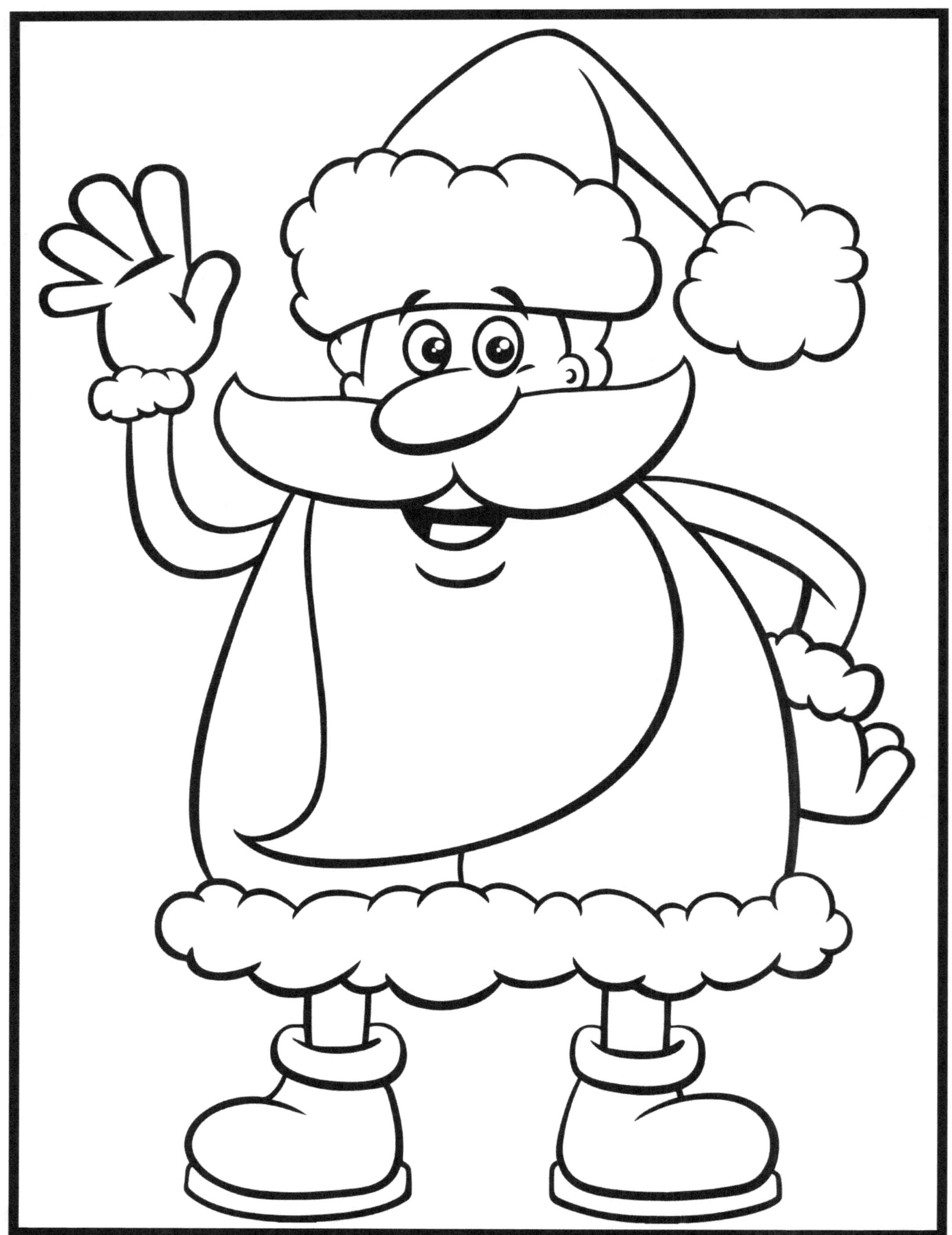

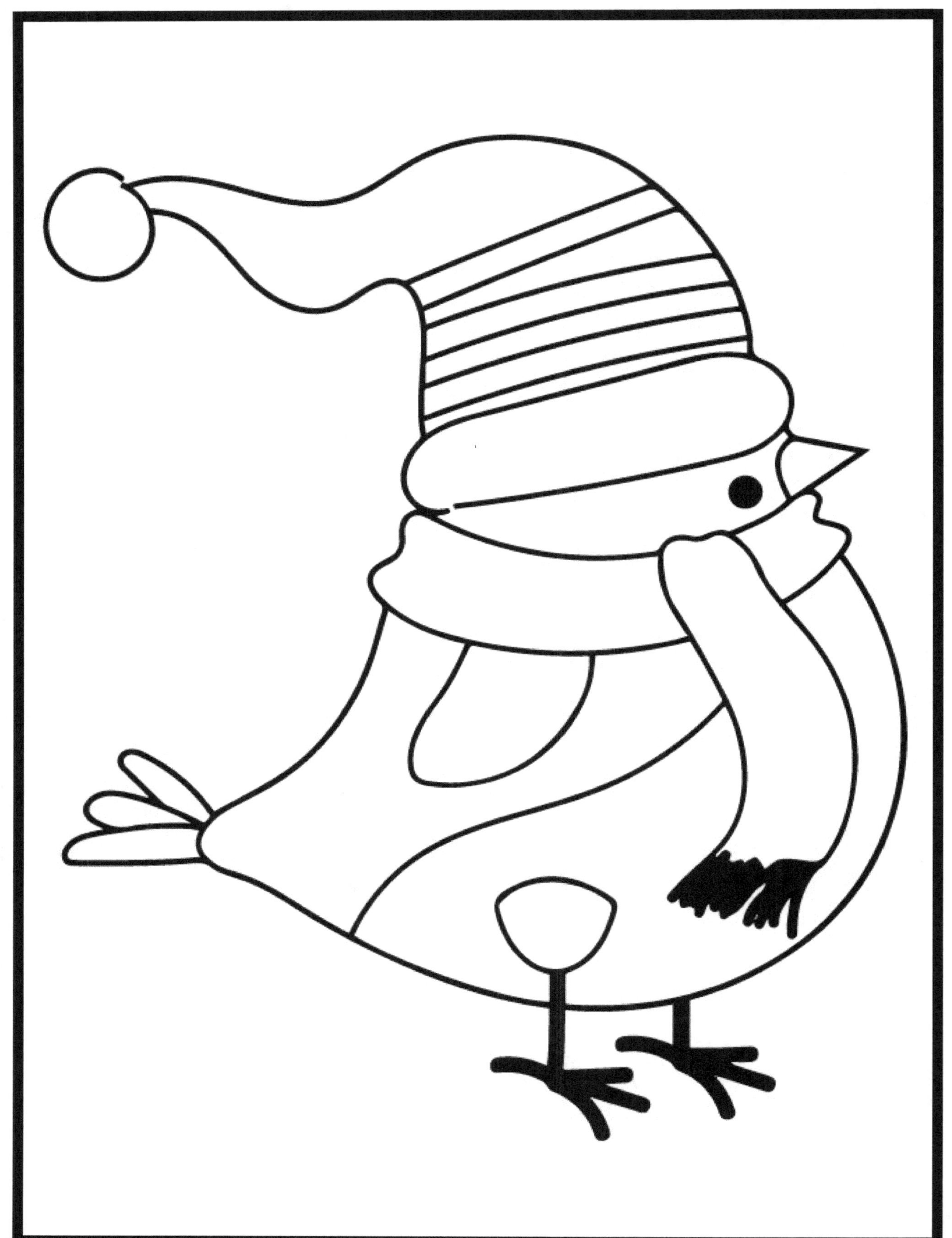

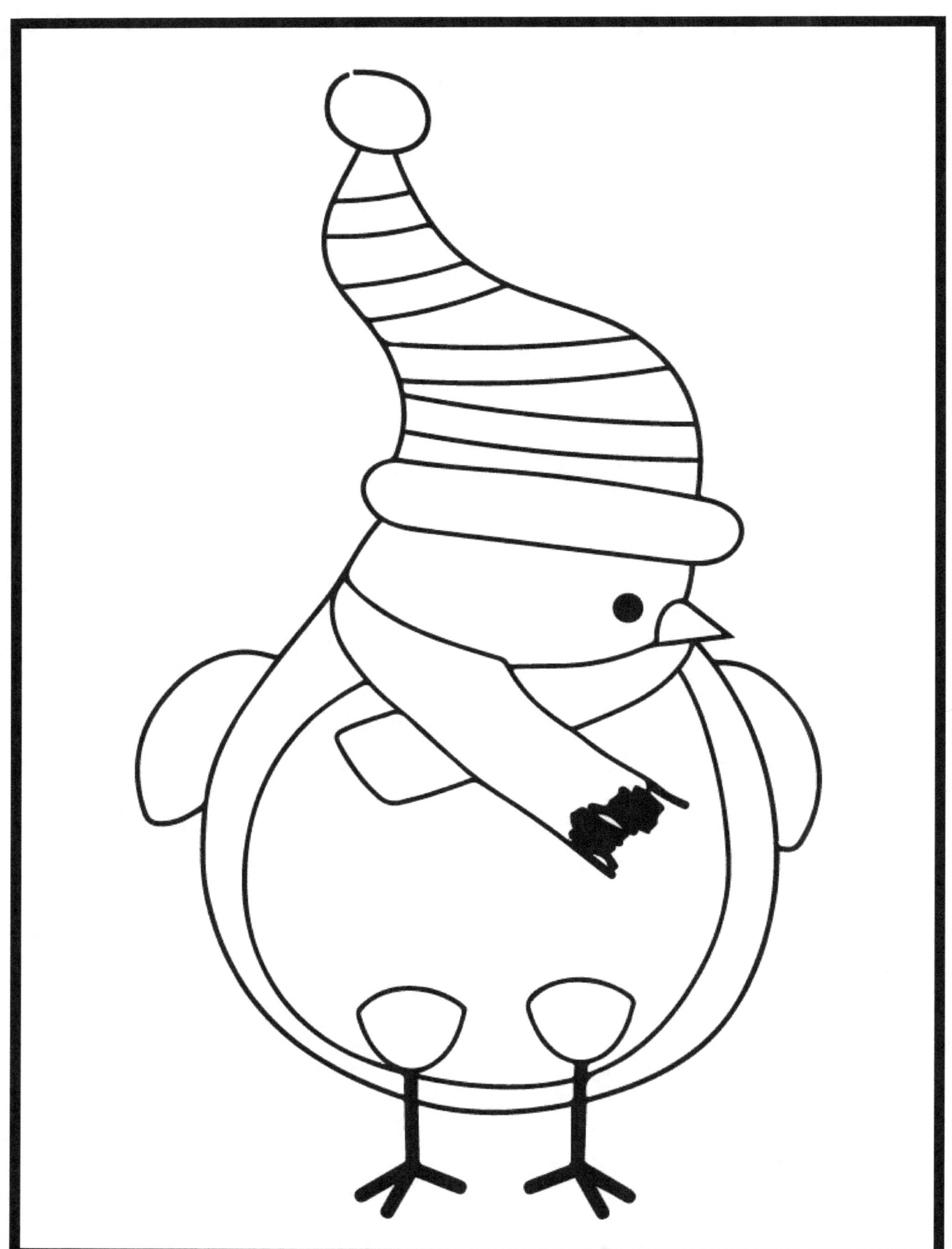

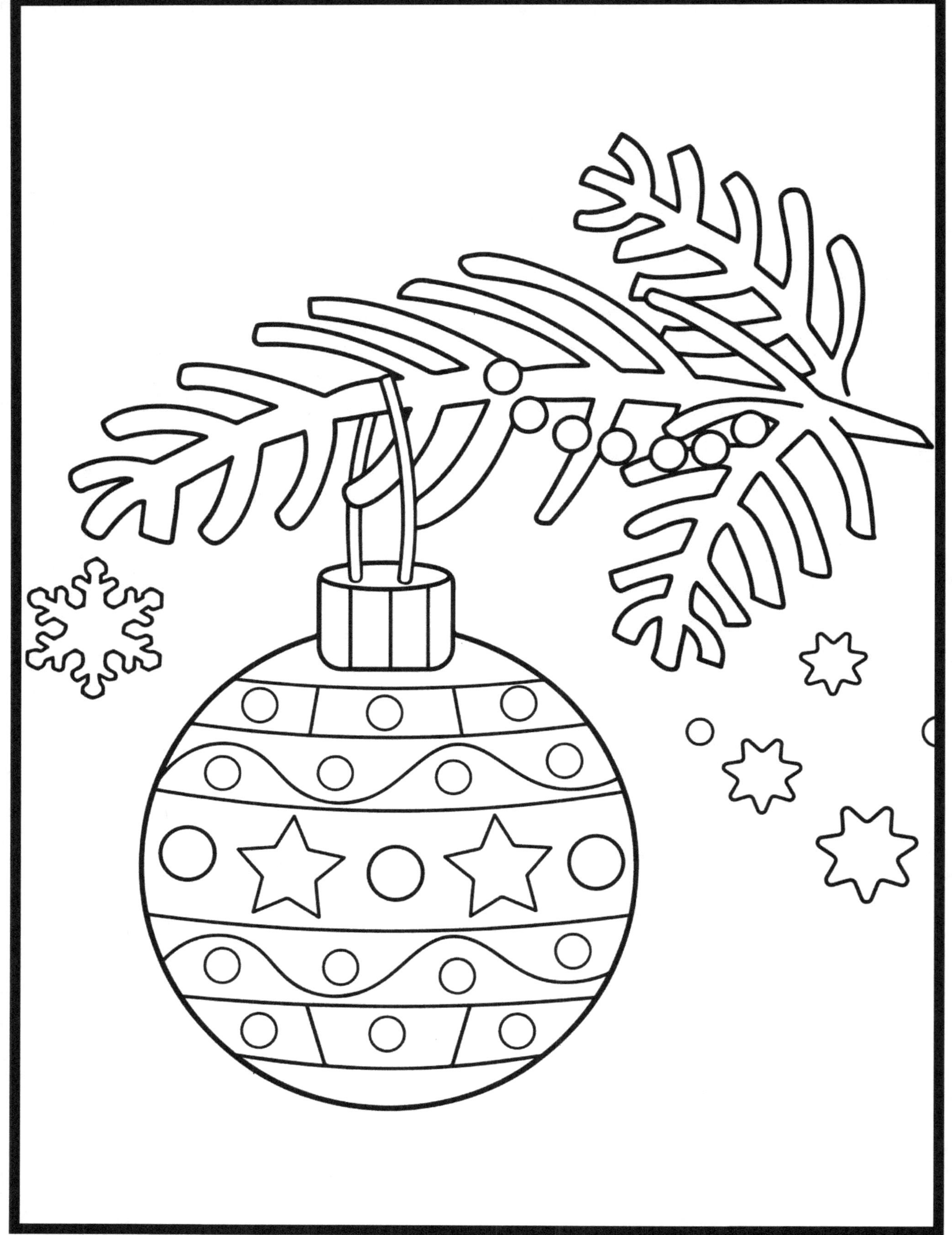

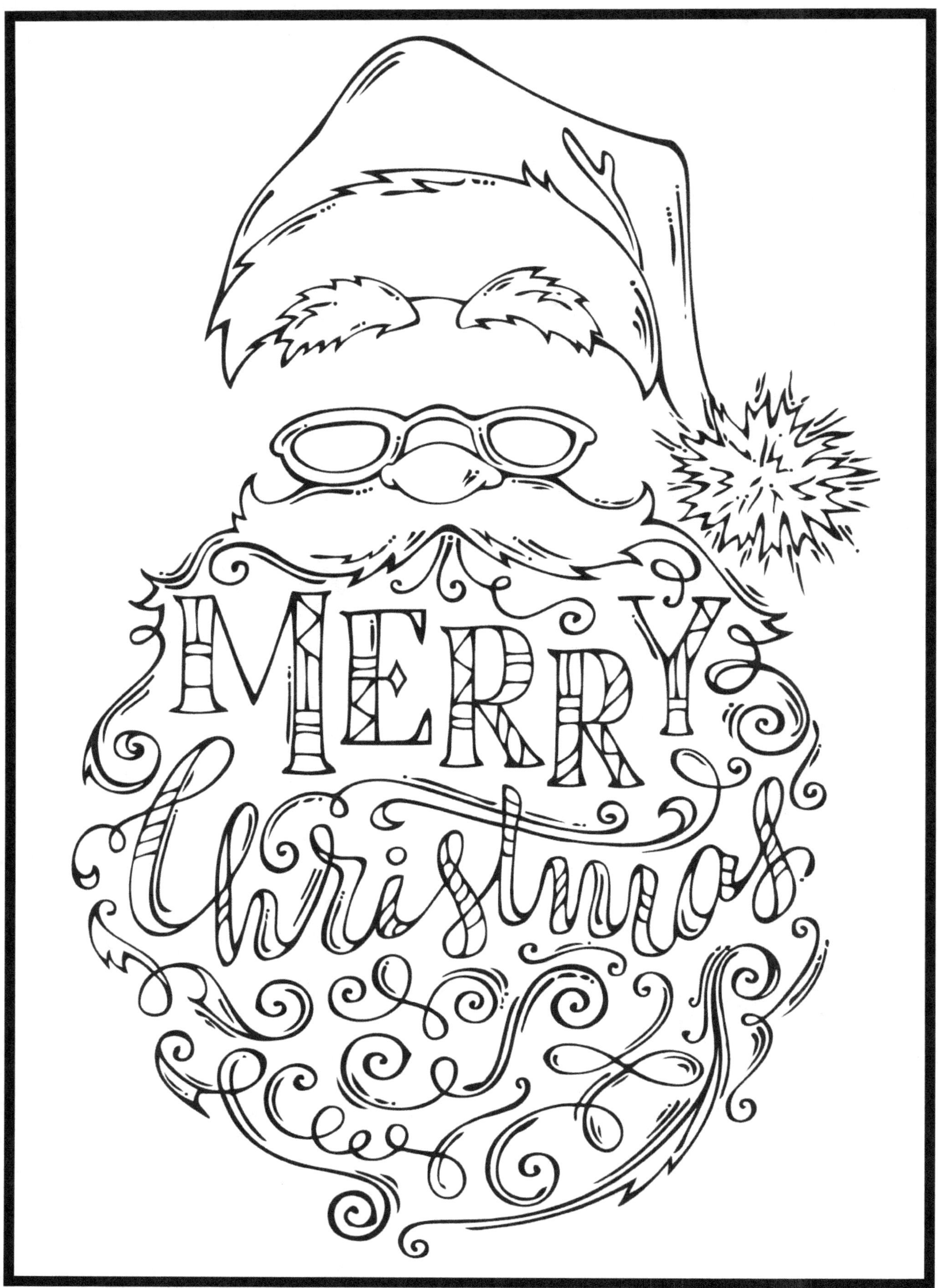

MERRY
Christmas

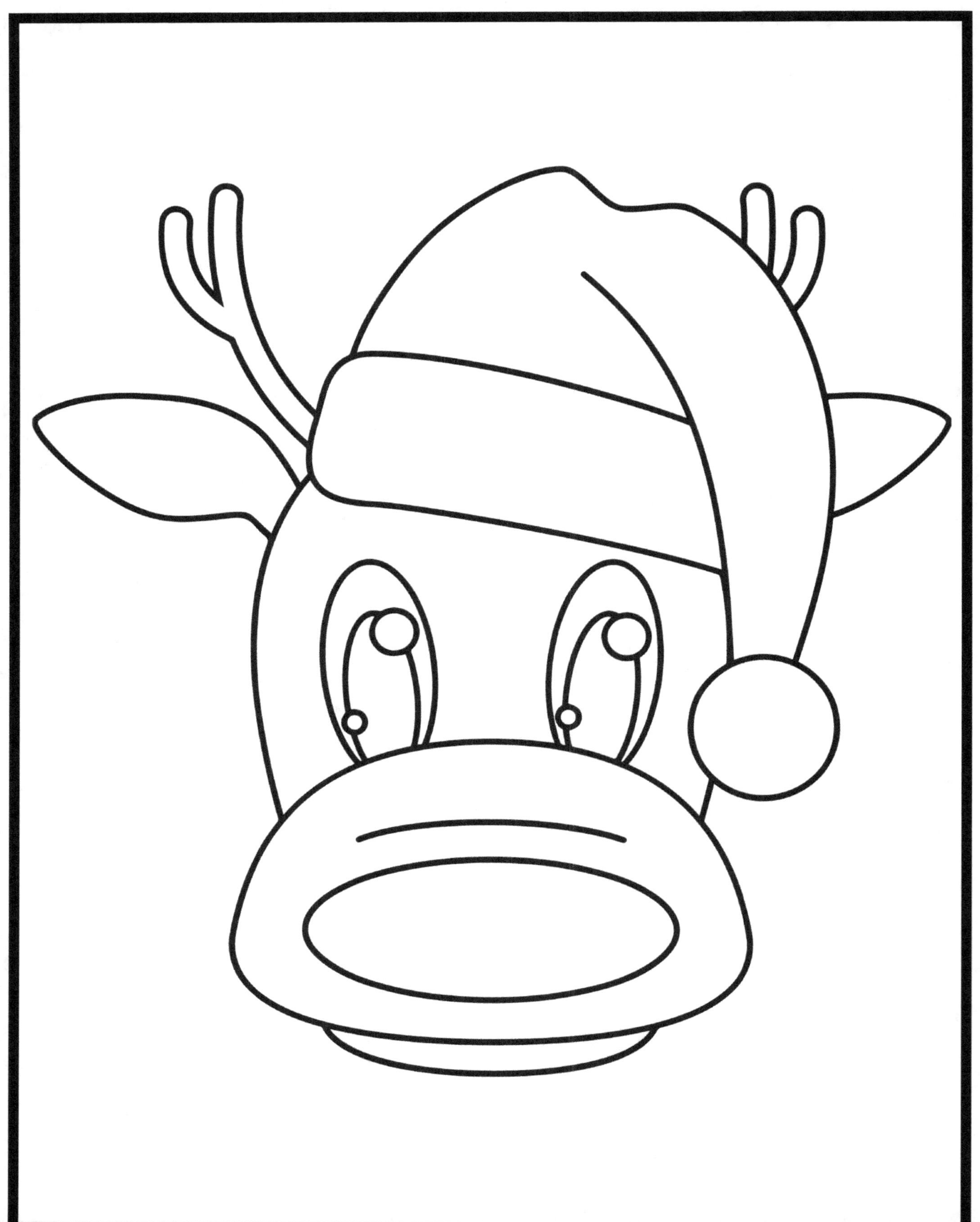

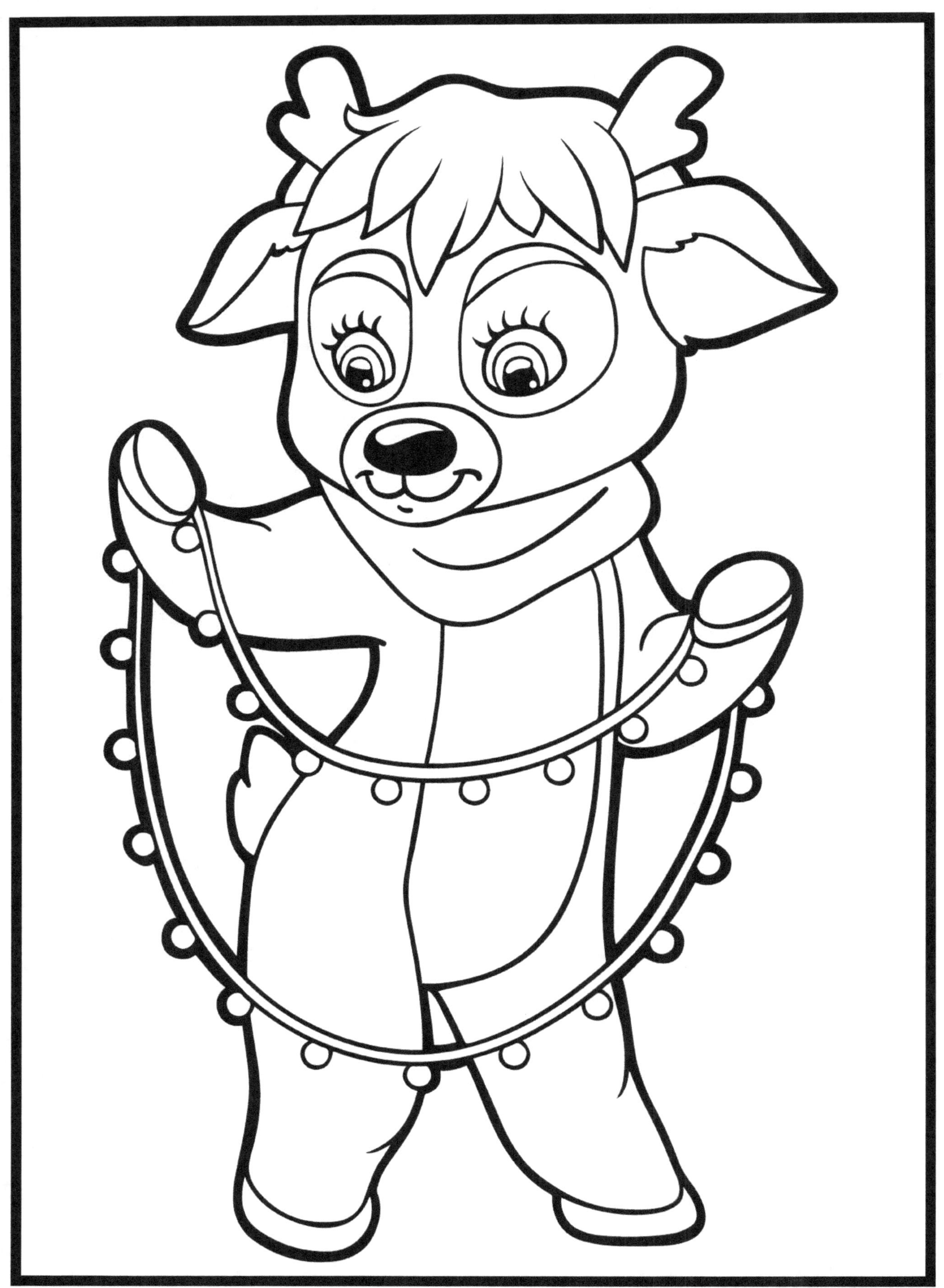

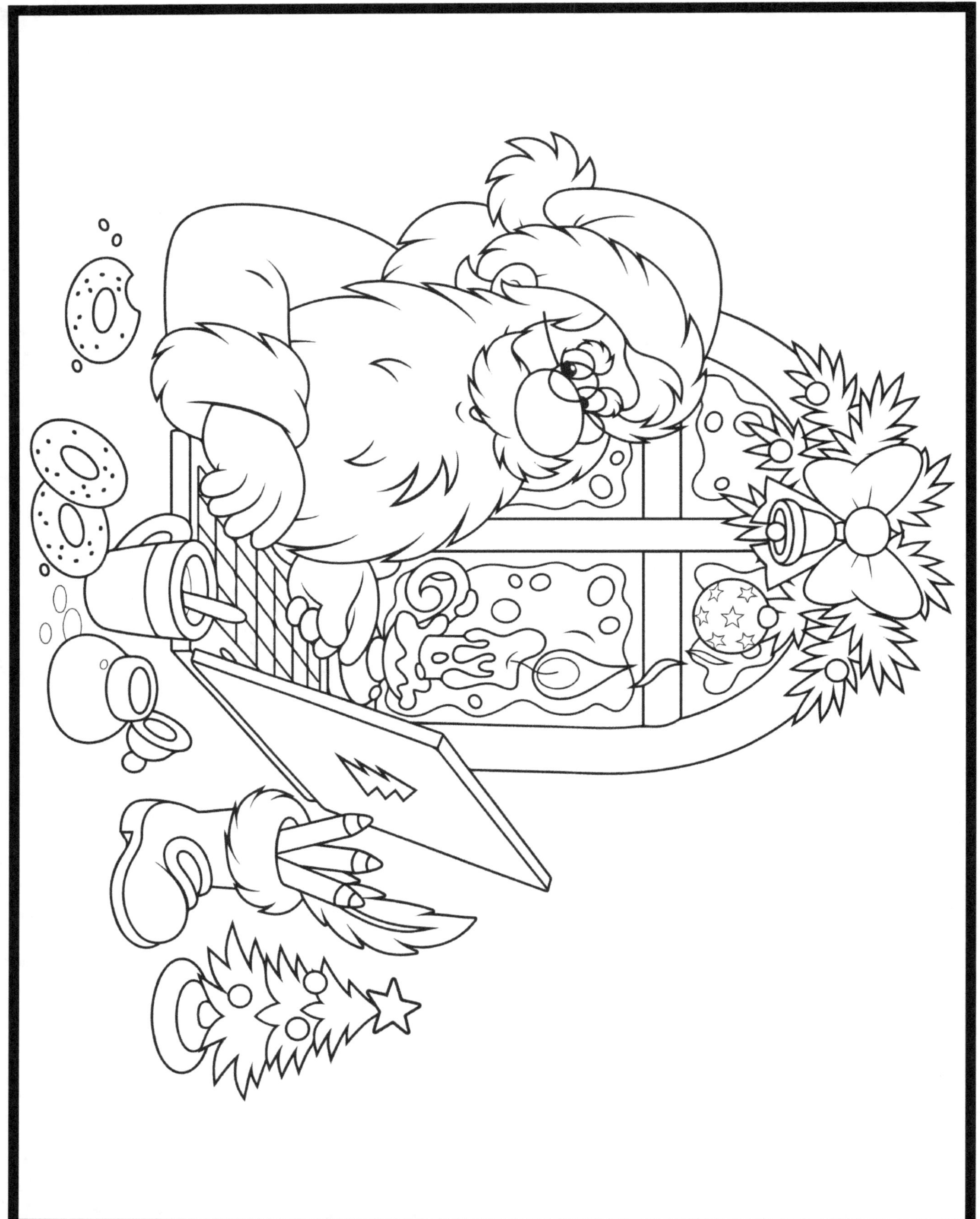

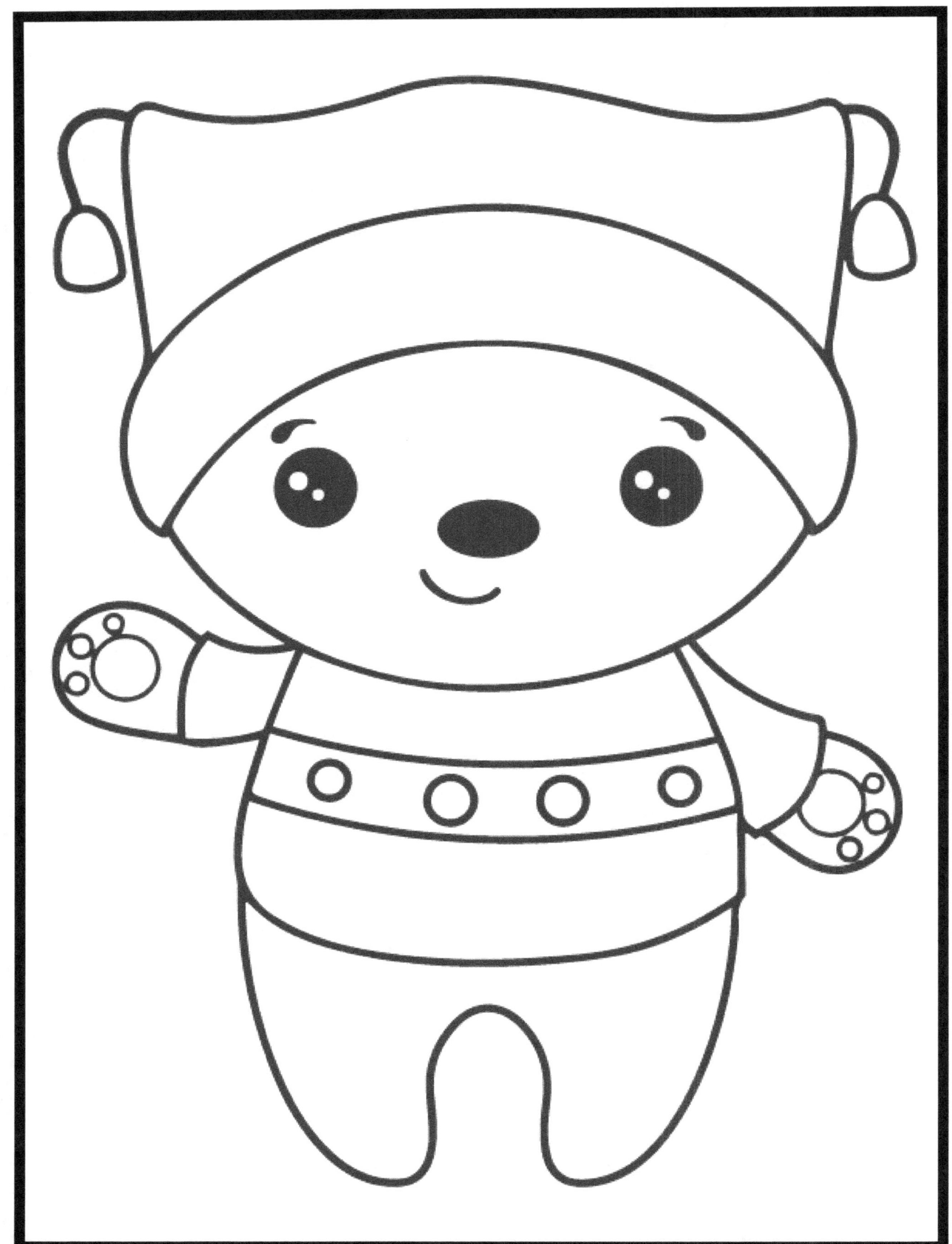

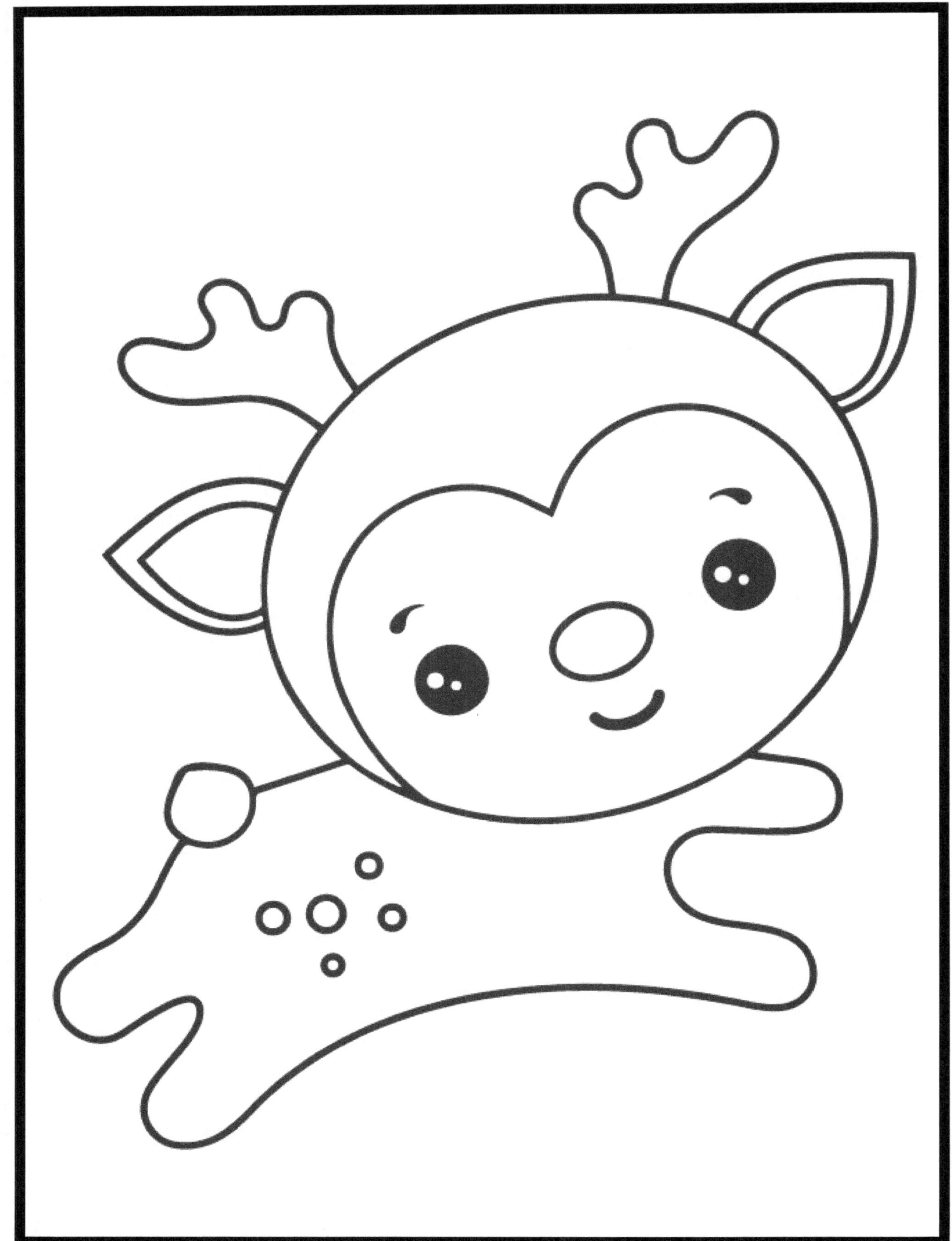

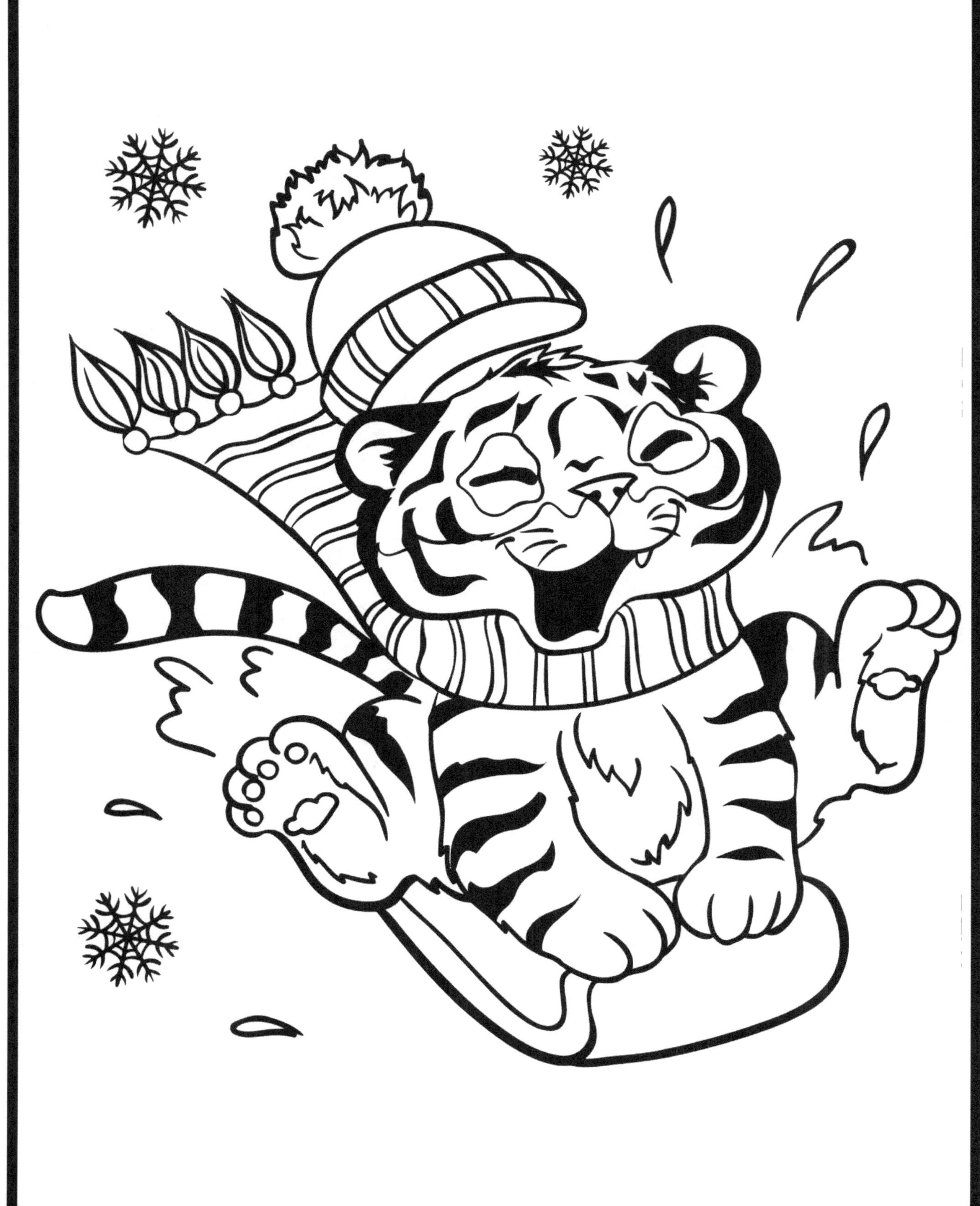

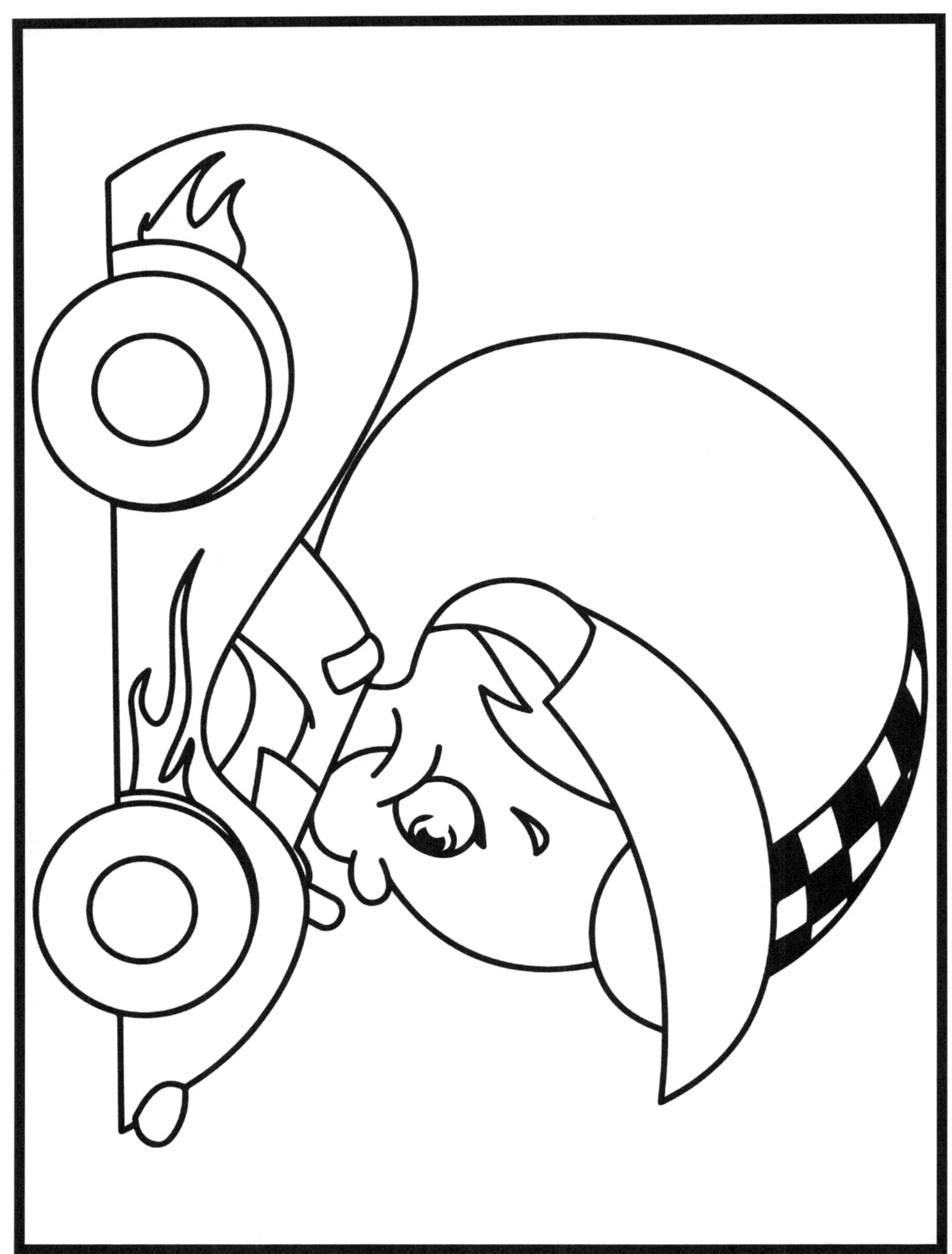

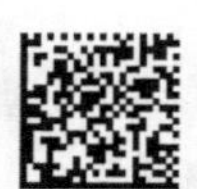

www.ingramcontent.com/pod-product-compliance
Lightning Source LLC
Chambersburg PA
CBHW081558270726
48657CB00029B/3377